Seeing With Your Ears

Seeing With Your Ears

❖

Spirituality
For Those Who Can't Believe

Art Lester

iUniverse, Inc.
New York Lincoln Shanghai

Seeing With Your Ears
Spirituality For Those Who Can't Believe

All Rights Reserved © 2003 by Art Lester

No part of this book may be reproduced or transmitted in any form or by any means, graphic, electronic, or mechanical, including photocopying, recording, taping, or by any information storage retrieval system, without the written permission of the publisher.

iUniverse, Inc.

For information address:
iUniverse, Inc.
2021 Pine Lake Road, Suite 100
Lincoln, NE 68512
www.iuniverse.com

ISBN: 0-595-28395-0 (pbk)
ISBN: 0-595-65782-6 (cloth)

Printed in the United States of America

Contents

Introduction: Seeing with Your Ears 1
Nothing is Merely Anything 7
Wake up! Pay Attention! 13
The Blessing of Uncertainty 19
Transformation for Beginners 24
Do You Have the Right to be Happy? 30
Hunting for Unicorns 36
Keeping up Appearances 42
Staying Alive 48
Learning from the Losers 54
Me and My Shadow 60
Tall Mast, Deep Keel 65
Getting Out of the Wu Wei 71
Eros the Healer 77
Dealing with Dragons 83
What is it Worth? 88
How to Be Good 94
The Trouble with Sandcastles 100
Trout Tickling for God 106

Feeding Your Angel 109
Welcome to the Lens Grinder's Shop 115
Letting Go 121
So What? 126
If There Was a God… 132
What I Wish I Had Said to Mary 138

Thanks

This book would have been impossible without the generosity of Chris Cooper-Hohn, the artistic talent of Dilys Bryon, the good sense and eagle eye of Barbara Williams and the patience of the members of Essex Unitarian Church, London. Finally, none of my books would have been written without Gilly.

Introduction:
Seeing with Your Ears

○ ○

"Trying to understand God is like trying to see with your ears."

—*Meher Baba*

Here's a question you don't hear too often: "Do you believe in God?"

For most of us, that sort of thing ends in secondary school. The only time you think about it after you're a grownup is in emergency wards and in the waiting rooms of police stations, or maybe when an engine stalls on your passenger jet. You may be surprised to hear that, even when I was a full-time Unitarian minister, hardly anyone asked me that.

Maybe because I conducted services every week, said prayers beside the graves of their relatives and sat next to them in hospital rooms, people assumed that the question was just too obvious. It's a good thing they didn't often ask, because the answer would have surprised them.

I might have tried to wriggle out of difficulty by saying, "Define your terms." But that would have been a sophistic copout, not what people in crisis need to hear. I might have tried saying nothing. Saying nothing at a key moment can be a useful tool. Or I might have tried to turn it back on them, the way your counsellor does: "What do *you* think?" But if I were being completely honest, I probably would have had to say, "No."

I would have meant that the God I supposed they were asking about had been rhetorically declared dead in 1966, on the front cover of *Time Magazine*. You remember the one I mean. He was an old white guy with a beard. He lived somewhere up there above the organ loft in your childhood church. He required a lot of flattery. He displayed a baffling amount of attitude toward certain meat products and certain days of the week. He was down on sex, too. And if you happened to be gay, you'd better wear rubber-soled shoes in case of lightning bolts.

I spent a fair amount of time with that God when I was a child. Having been told that he was constantly watching me, I spent many a night tossing in bed, trying to get him to ignore the small sins of the day. That was before I discovered girls. Come to think of it, that was about the time that God became terminally ill. By the time I was over my acne, I was over him, too.

The thing about that old God was that he was, as he admitted, *jealous*. Not only did he require you not to have any competing deities in mind, he wanted you to do one thing above all: *believe*. Offering little more than the threat of everlasting punishment and a few disputed miracles as evidence, he seemed to want you to freeze your mind. That meant that virtually everything you were coming in contact with that excited and made sense had to be mothballed or repudiated. You knew when you first made love that something wonderful was happening, something that would change your life forever, whether the experience was "successful" or not. You knew when you read Nietzsche, Marx or Darwin that ideas were like free airline tickets to places you had never imagined. You knew that your pet dog had a soul, too. You saw it in his eyes; never mind what the preacher said. All these things had the feel of truth about them. They were *real*. As they mounted up, you found you could not do that most important thing. You could not believe.

For many of us, that was that. The old man God had been overthrown. This produced a wonderful feeling of freedom. At first, that is. You were free to explore your mind and your sexuality. You could ignore ridiculous taboos about eating and drinking. You were free to laugh at or pity those who went around slavishly obeying outmoded and meaningless rules. That lasted until a point, perhaps around midlife, when the whole subject of meaning surfaces again.

When you reach a certain point in your career as a human being, the question stops being *what?* or *how?*, and starts becoming *why?* The insights of science and the security blanket of popular culture can do a lot with the first couple of questions, but they don't have much power with the third. Not that I didn't try. I was a good existentialist for a few years. This helped because there was no *why?* to deal with. The world was a great cosmic accident. There was no point in worrying about all that, because there *was no point*. You could behave with good faith toward the world and its other creatures or not. It didn't make a hell of a lot of difference, because when a lump appears where it shouldn't appear, or an eighteen-wheeler leaps the median strip, it's all over anyway. There was no point moaning about life and its events. The thing to do was be brave and get the most out of it. That idea was attractive then, and it's not too bad now.

In my case, two things interrupted my Sartreian dream. One was the persistence of a hunch that there was more to the equation than I was admitting. This hunch waxed and waned through a number of experiences, and frustrating though it was, had a very strong pull. I started reading non-Christian mystics and philosophers: Alan Watts, D.T Suzuki, and Herman Hesse. I took psychedelic drugs and meditated on straw mats and read the newspaper horoscope column. It was like that game of "hot and cold" that we played as children: when I got near something that felt like the truth, no matter how far-fetched it might seem, I got a feeling of warmth, and the hunch suspicion grew stronger. When I tried to analyse the experiences from an existential point of view, I felt cold.

I think I finally acquired a knack with all this experimentation. It is something which A.N. Whitehead called "the greatest intellectual achievement of modern humanity," the ability to suspend judgement. I felt I didn't have to reach an early conclusion; it was okay to just let ideas and feelings play around unsupervised in my mind, like unknown bacteria in a Petri dish. I was willing to trust that, sooner or later, they would find a way of sorting themselves out.

The second thing that helped me out of my certainty about there being no meaning in life was noticing that I was able to change my mind as new information appeared. Basing your conclusions on the already observed is fine: it's the heart of the scientific method. Reaching early conclusions and sticking with them, however, is not. New discoveries are made all the time. Theories of great physicists are overturned or amplified with boring regularity. Needing evidence is not the problem. Rushing to conclusions is. I became aware that the things I was not aware of vastly outnumbered the things that I knew. It seemed that I was going to have to be patient.

Finally, when I came into contact with the Indian spiritual master Meher Baba, I realised what had been bothering me all along. He said that asking to understand God was like asking for the privilege of seeing with your ears. This forced me to acknowledge that for quite a while I had been searching for a replacement for that God whose obituary was implied by *Time* back in 1966. It also meant that I was using the wrong tool for my search. The mind has its limitations. You could say, in fact, that the mind is entirely composed of limitations. If that is so, then forming an opinion is a risky business. Not so much when you're talking about investing in the stock market or calculating the numbers of rice grains in Asia, but when you're trying to explain the meaning of life, the universe and all that. Maybe the best thing to do is rely on your hunches. Maybe what I've come to think of as a hunch (you can substitute "intuition" or "inner voice" if you like) is a separate faculty that needs developing as much as the logical mind. Maybe we should try to be patient, and just wait and see.

The following essays all have one thing in common. They suggest a growing hunch about the ultimate meaning of things and how to recognise and support it. They are not limited to any one point of view or theology. You can think of them as a smorgasbord of ideas and images that will help feed some unnamed faculty we have so far left undeveloped. They are certainly not Christian, but the truths expressed through that great culture, particularly in its mystical tradition, are there to be used or discarded as needed. Lao Tse and Jesus, the Buddha and Rumi all sit together like friends at the dinner party, and that makes you the host.

Bon appetit!

Nothing is Merely Anything

Something happened recently, something of great cosmic significance. It is something that has never happened before in recorded history. I wonder if you know about it. I wouldn't know myself if I hadn't been reading the back pages of a newspaper on a long boring train journey. On page twenty-something, I saw a three-paragraph article that informed me that a star had exploded.

This star was 20,000 light years away, which means that when the explosion actually took place, virtually everything we know about the world hadn't happened yet. The energy of this explosion travelled through space at 186,000 miles per second while our ancestors lived in caves, when they began keeping domesticated animals, when they starting smelting bronze, then iron, when they built rude towns beside rivers, when they started speculating about the heavens, when Zoroaster and then Rama came along, while the Buddha sat under the Bo tree, through the whole long bittersweet history of Christianity, the formation of the nation state, the industrial revolution, and both world wars. This energy was still travelling during our births and all through our lives. It reached the Pacific Ocean one night while we were sleeping.

The article said that the energy of this explosion penetrated to within fifty kilometres of the Earth's surface before being absorbed by that wonderful womb of gases we call the atmosphere. A good thing it did, because it was great enough, according to scientists, to provide all the energy Earth will need, every BTU for cooking, every torch beam and headlamp, every electric toothbrush, for a billion years. That's right, a billion years, probably longer than we've got left. They said that the magnetic energy alone was great enough thirty miles above

Hawaii to snatch the car keys out of your pocket at a distance halfway to the moon. But we hardly noticed it.

I sat and re-read the article. I felt that I should rush to a telephone and tell somebody about it. A star has exploded! How could we be more interested in reading about what latest crisis was going to pose a threat or what, if we added it to our diets, would make us live forever? And then the story moved to page twenty-six in my own mind, behind recipes for cauliflower soup and overdue telephone bills, and all the wonder of it just oozed away.

Perhaps it's all just too much for the human mind to absorb. Perhaps we were designed to pay attention only to the near, the next and the needful, our scope of concern no greater than the ring of illumination from our campfires or the line of sight from the highest hill. That's probably why a massive flood in Bangladesh that has made 25 million people homeless isn't front page news. It's too much, too far away for little us.

And yet, every once in a while something penetrates the comfortable bandages we have wrapped our heads in and breaks up, for an instant, the "psychic numbing" from which people like James Hillman say we suffer. I had such a moment on the train. I felt electrified for a brief instant. As my attention zoomed out into the cosmos, I felt myself shrinking to the size of a molecule. I felt wonder at the sheer immensity of things, a kind of dread or fear, and, in the same instant, a little prayer was born. The prayer was in part a plea for protection because I was so small and insignificant and vulnerable, in part a chest-swelling appreciation for the universe and its marvels, and finally something else: an undeniable feeling of reverence. One word sums all this up: *awe*.

Awe means "an emotion compounded of dread, veneration and wonder inspired by authority, or by something sacred or sublime." It is something we don't often encounter these days. We're too wrapped up in reassuring scientific statements for that. A hurricane is easily explained as a meteorological phenomenon, not the wrath of God.

Heart attacks are preventable and even correctable with diet and exercise and surgery, no longer marking the dreaded arrival of the Grim Reaper with his little black book of appointments. Even a smile can be explained and then filed away as a mere physiological reaction. It seems that we won't be content until every irrational anxiety has its pharmacological remedy, every occurrence of nature its predictable response. As for a star blowing up a long way from here...well, that's *merely* a supernova, just as the star of Bethlehem probably was. No big deal, really.

This rationalising tendency of ours has its good points. When we reduce everything to *mere* phenomena, we get rid of irrational fear, and that's probably more comfortable. The problem is, we also get rid of the other elements of the word *awe*, the parts about veneration and wonder, that all-too-infrequent glimpse of "something sacred and sublime." It makes me wonder, "Were we made to go about mouthing that magic word *merely* about everything? Has the life-giving baby within us, full of wonder and reverence, been chucked out with the bath water of superstitious fear?"

The ancient project of religion has always depended upon a copious supply of awe. Philosophers of the subject have usually maintained that the first acts of propitiation of the gods probably happened during a thunderstorm, when Thor was hurling lightning bolts and Manitou was weeping. Such tales evolved along with us, and awe was our constant companion. The Old Testament is full of them: city walls tumbling, seas parting, mighty winds and plagues of frogs—the list is endless. All this was capable of making people feel dread and reverence, the *sine qua non* of worship. Dread and reverence are inconvenient in a world of rationality and progress; they get replaced by depression (treatable with Prozac) and lots of debunking information (available on the Internet). All this makes for hard times for good old religion—without dread and awe, who needs it? But if we have a hunch that living without awe is not necessarily a good thing, where on earth do we find it?

I once saw a TV programme that explained the series of mind-blowing events that made Pharaoh let Moses and his band of Israelites get out of Egypt. It seems that many of these plagues—red river water, millions of frogs, animal illnesses and so on—probably really happened. How they know that is a marvel in itself. The bad news is—you guessed it—it was all *merely* the result of an increase in a certain known microorganism. Hooray! Saved again by the scientists, who give us back Biblical wonder with one hand, and then remove it with the other. What Moses needed was not a forty-year trek through the Middle East, but a few buckets of antibiotic powder available from your nearest drugstore. The ability to explain away things is wonderful, but it's like a kind of steroid injection into the soul of the culture: it makes us stronger and weaker at the same time.

Perhaps what we need to do is change the historical lenses we have been wearing. If we can no longer depend upon being overwhelmed by miracles from on high, we must learn to find them in the smallest of things. For me, finding the Nile River bacterium doesn't mean that awe goes out the window; it means that we have to look for it in unaccustomed places, even with a microscope. The bug that turned Pharaoh's river red isn't *merely* anything. It is a miracle of a different sort. And I need to find not explanations, but the lost wonder of the primitive inside me.

When people ask, as they properly should, what the purpose of a church is these days, when everything is on course to be handled by scientific research, I think I have an answer. If religion once depended upon an encounter with *awe*, then we must use religion to find it again. How about this: we could start an *awe* shop, right in the middle of a local shopping mall. We could call it 24-Hour Awe Recovery Service. "We doze, but never close." Motto: "Nothing Is *Merely* Anything." Awe is still around; we just need a little help finding it.

Ask any new set of parents about *awe*. Somebody has recently come to join them, somebody whom they did not know, but who is to become a central figure in their lives. This new friend arrived with a complete set of characteristics. Not just hair and teeth and fingernails, but with a soul as large and full of hunger for the world as we are. All the medical language in the world, all the ultra-sound and amniocentesis there is can't predict what this little person will be like. There will be a moment, when the parents gaze into this face and—miracle!—the little face gazes back, and all the explanations about genes and microbiology will simply melt away.

I think the tendency to awe has more to do with a state of mind than with any outside events. I think awe can be cultivated, through the unwinding of the psychic bandages we have installed in this frenetic age. I think poets have this gift; mystics and artists, too. I think we have it as children, and it is not that it is beaten out of us, but that, as we age, we make small compromises with the world. We say, in effect, if you just won't make me feel dread, then I'll give up feeling wonder. Only sometimes, as when a baby is born, we will risk the profundity of that feeling, and for a little while we'll admit that we are subject to the universe, to both its kind and its terrifying faces. We need to be a little bolder. We need to rely a bit more on faith in the deep-down final all-rightness of things that will let us open up to the truth. Because, by the way, isn't that what we are after?

We could start today, if we wanted to. We could, like Thich Nhat Hanh, sit and peel and eat a banana, really experiencing it as we do, paying attention to its uniqueness in a universe of bananas, the subtlety of its flavour, the smoothness of its peel, the pleasure of its little stringy bits inside. We could imagine who cut it, carried it, cleaned it, removed the tarantulas from it, shipped it, sold it; we could learn a lot from a banana if we wished. I'm not kidding. At the very least we could ignore its calorie count and its potassium content and just be there with it. Or we could look at someone who is by now so familiar to us that we hardly notice them any more and pay the same sort of attention to them that Hanh did to his banana.

And, no, we don't want to go around being overawed all the time. We can't stand in rapt wonder every time a street light changes or be dazzled by all the leaves in the park. We would go around like imbeciles, jaw perpetually dropped and unable to function. Some psychic numbing is necessary; we just don't want to let it rule us.

The Bible claims that the God the Israelites sought wasn't just there in the rushing wind or the shaking of the earth. He also had his place in the "still small voice"—read: the insignificant, the trivial, and the *mere*. But the still small voice is hard to hear, what with the drumbeat of excitement and the earplugs of complacency to contend with. If we are to reclaim our ability to experience awe, it will be because we have made the effort. We are too old and wise to depend upon red rivers these days—somebody will just find a bacterium and spoil it. We need to go to the heart of things, risking the fears that are the admission price, just as have the sages of all time. It is in these places, stripped of unnecessary protection, that we begin to live as we should. We are not visitors here, you know. This is our universe, scary and wonderful place that it is. It's our own home address. It's about time we started looking at it, risking fear, but gaining awe.

Wake up! Pay Attention!

Have you ever had this experience? You're driving down a highway in the afternoon after a big lunch, a long monotonous highway, with nothing but the drone of tires on concrete to listen to. You begin to feel sleepy, so you open the window to get some fresh air. Perhaps you hum a little tune. A few minutes later, you realise that you have actually been asleep for a few microseconds. The car has swerved just a little. It is worrying. You resolve that you are going to snap out of it, so you sit upright in your seat, give yourself a little slap on both cheeks. A few minutes later it happens again. You are in danger of going to sleep at the wheel. A little *frisson* of fear injects some adrenaline into your system, and you feel momentarily alert.

"There, that's better," you say. The next exit comes and goes, and now you are sure that you will stay awake. Five minutes later a horn blast from an articulated lorry jars you out of a dream. You were drifting into his lane, hands on the wheel, eyes open but glazed, foot on the accelerator, but sound asleep. Now there's nothing for it but to stop at the next service station. Despite your resolve, you are falling asleep, a danger to yourself and everyone else.

Anybody who has ever had that experience knows that we are only partially in control of our lives. It is almost as if there are two of us in one body, the mental one who knows that it is vital to remain awake at the wheel, and the biological one, inclined to have forty winks whenever possible. P.D. Ouspensky, writing about Georges Gurdjieff's techniques for self-realisation, once pointed out that there are several fragmented selves within everybody. He gave the example of someone driving a car. This process is automatic: you steer and brake without really thinking about it unless something unusual happens. But at the same time, this man is on his way to visit his family, so he's thinking about them, picturing their faces and anticipating the meal they'll have ready. Also, he has a cavity in a molar that's bothering him slightly, so he's rubbing his jaw, aware of the pain.

Ouspensky wanted to alert us to the fact that there is not just one of us, but three or more. The being we are pleased to call "I" is actually more like "us." It seems that the ordinary self is a little amorphous and diffused; it leaks out of the world of the present and the physical into the worlds of imagination and dream. Our official selves may be headed in one direction while our biological and fantasy centres are going in another. Focussing the diverse "small" self into one being was an important part of the spiritual discipline that Gurdjieff referred to as "The Work." Exercises were employed to focus and intensify awareness through a process of self-observation. This included exercises of motion and dance, which came in a direct line from Sufism and the dervish dancing of masters like Rumi.

This process is visible in many of the great faith traditions. In Zen Buddhism, the practice of meditation is to focus the attention of the adherent on the real and the present, to bring together the disparate elements of the self. The injunction to what Buddhists call "mindfulness in all things" has at its root the idea that in order to become liberated one must become more conscious, and that in order to become more conscious, one must pay attention. Through paying attention, one arrives fully in the *now*—the *eternal now* as it is often called. And this, as so many mystics and sages have insisted, is the point where "time touches eternity."

Our lack of attention is well known to psychologists. I read once that the attention span of an average adult in listening is about nine minutes. After a short time, the mind wanders, down into the body and out into fantasy. Ask any preacher and they'll tell you that sometimes the best satisfaction available from a sermon is being able to provide a few catnaps for tired parishioners.

It is not just lack of sleep that keeps us from paying attention. There is a story about a policeman investigating the theft of a painting from a museum. A guard had been posted continuously outside the gallery door all the day of the crime; he swore that no one had entered or left the room where the painting was hung. The detective said, "Are you absolutely sure that nobody went through this door?" The guard responded, "That's right, no one at all. Absolutely no one." Then he added, "Well, except for the postman." He was proving that the ordinary passes not over, but under, our heads. The practice of focussing on the ordinary, the real, and the present is a high discipline that few of us know how to perform. The monotony of the motorway, the tedium of routine, the ordinariness of our lives means that we often miss important things.

When I studied rural development for the Third World, I was lucky to come across the work of Paolo Freire, the Brazilian educator and philosopher. Freire's work had been adapted to village situations, where the tangle of life as a poor person had for many years frustrated development workers. The old idea was to drive up to a village in your Jeep, bring out a clipboard and talk to a few people, asking them about their problems. Workers found that everybody had the same problems: no money, no cars, no jobs. This was all true of course, but it did little to suggest ways forward.

Freire developed the technique of moving into the village, perhaps on some pretext like measuring rainfall, and then just *listening* for a year or so. Listening where people met, at the river where women beat the clothing on the rocks, say, or in the village saloon after work. What you were listening for were those things that keep coming up in people's conversation, things that are so ordinary that you might otherwise fail to notice them at all. A famous example is the one about football uniforms.

In a desperately poor refugee relocation camp in northern Uganda, where children died in droves from diarrhoea and people went blind from lack of vitamin A, a pair of workers noticed that the most important topic of conversation was football shirts. It seems that there were four teams forming to play football on a scrubby pitch near the camp. Everybody knew the players and the scores. The people longed, not for medicine or education—both were clearly out of the question—but for some way of identifying the teams. The workers had access to a small grant from the Dutch government. With great reluctance, being Freirian advocates, they delivered the funds to a small group of women who could sew. The women bought cloth and sewed the shirts in four primary colours; the players wore them, and a minor miracle of community development took place. The football league became the core of the self-help movement in the camp, which led on to schools and clinics. The identity with the league provided the momentum workers had waited for in vain, the momentum that made passive victims into active participants in life. This was possible because the workers paid attention. The people themselves may not have known they were formulating a solution; they just knew what they liked.

When a patient presents him or herself to a psychotherapist, something similar happens. The "presenting issue" may be about insomnia, a phobia concerning spiders, or some such thing. The skilful therapist knows that our lives are full to bursting with clues about what we need to do, but we can't see them. What we see is a forest of small emergencies that aren't related to the big picture. It is the role of the psychotherapist to listen on two levels: the one where the patient is aware and the one where he or she is not aware. Patterns can be discerned that give helpful directions for growth; it is the job of the therapist to notice them, to pay attention. A phrase may repeatedly crop up in the patient's speech, or a certain tendency to react in a similar way in very different situations.

For instance a woman might have tripped and sprained her ankle when crossing the street. She may be accident-prone. It would be simple to say that she's "seeking attention," and perhaps that's so. But a sensitive ear can learn that she was crossing the street to avoid passing a shop window where they sell dolls. She does this every day. One day she falls. The right questions are about the dolls that remind her of her bitter childhood, not about the height of her heels or the degree of wetness of the pavement. We go around handing out clues to our secret lives without seeing them, virtually wearing placards that, if we bothered to read them, would give all the direction and centredness that our fractured lives require. If we paid attention.

Paying attention has another form. In the Hindu path, one of the high yogas is called Bhakti yoga, or the path of devotion. In this practice the attempt is to remember God—as always, use your own image—in every moment. I have some Sufi friends who repeat one of the names of God every time they look at their wristwatches. The idea is that the self has very little centre and needs to be focussed. If you see God as the ultimate reality, then the proper orientation of life is toward that goal. "High resolve," as Howard Thurman puts it. In some forms of Eastern religion, if you can remember to say the name of God when breathing your last, liberation will follow. This is because, in your last moments, you are likely to be thinking about your pain, unpaid taxes or the nurse's ankles. Lack of focus is hard to overcome, even at the moment of truth.

I have come to believe that we're all stuck in a kind of silly irony. Writings in the religious traditions are full of people straining to communicate with God. Like trying to tune in a fuzzy channel on a TV set. Like the "dark night of the soul" when God's cell phone number is engaged and you can't get through. Trying to pray when we cannot believe, like whistling into the wind. Meanwhile, say some, through all this, God is trying to communicate with us; it is we who are otherwise engaged. Clues multiply all around us, but we ignore them, lacking the quality of attentiveness. Our prayers, emerging murkily from the mixed soup of our consciousness, are barely formed before they dissipate and disappear. It is a little like the Boy Scout who tries desperately to light a fire with two sticks and asks his friend to hold a candle nearby so that he can see. The fire is already there; we don't need to kindle it.

If God, as so many of the sages have said, is trying—no, *straining*—in our direction at every moment, maybe we should give up our struggle and start paying attention. We don't need to invent God if He is inventing us. What we need to do is pay attention, to wake up from our self-deluding fog of busyness and become present at the occasion.

Our lives are full of incidents and people that may seem irrelevant. Is your TV on the blink, your computer crashed? And that annoying neighbour catches your eye across the fence and bores you with irrelevant chat for an hour. To make things worse, you've got to have a root canal and you don't like the hair growing out of the dentist's ears. And more tedium and unnoticeable trivia arrives every day. We can't see all these as envoys of the truth because we're not awake. Meanwhile, the pavement is strewn with miracles which we carefully avoid, being too busy or too bored to notice.

Yes, it's time for a wake up call. Time to notice what we screen out all the time. Time to understand that every tiny bit of our lives, no matter how seemingly irrelevant may be a Rosetta stone for the scrambled hieroglyphs of our lives. It could just be that everything is important, more important than we know.

The Blessing of Uncertainty

When I tell people what I do, the situation often becomes strained. It seems that it's not so much a question of my disapproving of their language or behaviour, but that I might be a member of some weird cult. That's one of the good and wise things about non-religious people: they have a healthy mistrust of cults and sects. It does no good to tell them how open-minded I am, how tolerant I am of other religions, or even how little connection I have to traditional Christianity. The wisdom of the worldly agnostic makes them wary of believers, full stop. And you know what? I can't blame them.

Not long ago *The Guardian* ran a long article about the hottest new movement within the mainstream churches—the Alpha Programme. What began as a small adult study group in the Anglican Church has become a world-wide phenomenon, spreading to 119 countries and claiming to have converted over a million people to Christianity. The epicentre of this phenomenon in Britain is a church called Holy Trinity, Brompton, where a charismatic priest has overturned the good old stuffy vicar image and made many C of E churches the home of "born again believers."

The programme is a little like most adult religious education courses. I believe it lasts twelve weeks, with one weekday evening session and one final weekend retreat. The style is like that of what many of us have come to know as facilitated group work, a method arising from Freudian group analysis and the encounter groups of psychologists like Carl Rogers. Participants sit together and are led through a series of Bible readings, prayers and the sharing of personal experiences. By all accounts, people experience "bonding" with each other and acquire a particular affection for the charismatic leader, in a way that seems very close to what is called "transference" in psychotherapy. Many people feel love for him and seem to want to please and impress him as you would a parent. Their insights at the end of the course are very much like his ideas: a hard version of Christian doctrine that includes Hell, the Devil and the end of the world.

None of this is mysterious to those of us who have had training in group therapy or facilitation. There are processes, mostly unconscious ones, which make the most cynical and wary of us subject to feelings of elevation and susceptible to unconscious suggestions from a group leader. In fact, a major part of training in these skills consists of avoiding this effect, or a least using it to free the perceptions of participants. It is near to being a moral absolute, and the institution of supervision has this as its main aim.

You can take almost any group of people for a weekend and produce an experience of bonding. I know this because it has happened to me. When I was twelve years old, I got "saved" for the first time. Don't laugh; if it's never happened to you I feel sorry for you. There was this extremely charismatic preacher who ran a ministry called "Sermons from Science." He was at the local high school for a run of five nights. One Tuesday I went with Mike Fields and his family. The preacher showed slides of a mastodon found frozen in an ice cap with a daisy in his mouth, proving, somehow, that the flood of the Bible had really happened. He took me through interlocking circles of unreason until I was somehow convinced that he had made me born again. When he asked those who had been saved to come forward, up I went. We were shown into a classroom where we were prayed over and saved. Our names and addresses were entered in a registry.

This took about an hour. Meanwhile, Mike and Mr. and Mrs. Fields, unsaved, sat in their car and fumed. I was embarrassed when I finally got into their car, but, God help me, I must have thought their ill humour was the work of the Devil. I stayed saved until Wednesday of the following week, and I've never forgotten it. For years my parents got mail from the reverend's mission, declaring imminent doom and asking for money for the Lord's work. Meanwhile, I was having my normal introduction to the Devil as a teenager and cheerfully forgot about my immortal soul. But I have always remembered the powerful effect that a certain kind of—yes—brainwashing can have over you.

The Alpha Programme has become more or less respectable in the C of E. Even the grumbling of a few traditionalists is taken to be sour grapes. The course has filled a lot of formerly empty pews, and those who measure the Lord's work by the "bums on seats" method have learned to swallow their bile. A million converts, mostly among the "unchurched," can't be sneered at. Or can it?

Maybe we could start an Omega Programme or something like that. Here's how it might work. First, we'd have to scare the hell out of people. That's not too hard these days, when all the old values that kept our parents going have been drowned in a sea of relativity. We could frighten people with the wrath of God—call down AIDS as a divine punishment, or find some half-baked Biblical quotation that indicates the imminent end of the world. We could trot out the Devil from his well-deserved retirement, make him gay or Muslim, for example. There are a lot of things we could do. But the effect would be to heat up the existential dread we all feel sometimes—fears about cancer, loneliness, bankruptcy—and encourage a mistrustful attitude toward the world. We could forget about the environment and global injustice, because all that would have a new name—Satan. Every cult needs an enemy.

Once everybody was good and scared, we could offer a way out. We could draw a circle in the sand around us. Everybody inside would be safe, but more than that, they would be special. We could give each other knowing glances when confronted by an unbeliever, and exercise Christian charity towards them. We could invent code words and slogans and use them like magic charms to keep reason at bay. Every good cult needs to provide a sense of being special.

The third thing we would need would be a substitute high for the booze, sex and tobacco we'd left behind. That would mean being "spirit filled." To do this, you need sad music that gradually becomes ecstatic. You need people to confess and share their encounters with the Devil out loud. We could encourage people to re-discover an ancient secret language and start speaking in tongues, but sensibly—after the collection. We'd get high every Sunday, and on Wednesday evenings too. Every good cult has to be able to get its adherents high.

There is one more ingredient we would have to add. It's called "belief." Knowing that our minds are twisted by the Devil, we would have to make them shut up. When one of us asked, as a recent letter writer to *The Guardian* did, if all homosexuals really had to go to Hell, we'd pray for their unbelief with them until the questions stopped. Gradually, with the aid of music and the loving attentions of the preacher, we'd get over silly questions and just re-shape our minds until the truth resembled the permitted facts. We could take our pick from among a number of creeds, and pity the Unitarians and Quakers who don't have one.

If I have been sounding a little intolerant, forgive me. One of the things that makes me mad is when people shape truth to fit their agendas. I feel the same way about Hitler youth camps and the CIA. I'm a tolerant person, but when somebody kidnaps a great teacher like Jesus of Nazareth and holds him hostage in their logic-free cells, I tend to lose my temper. When they make God into a spiteful experimenter with human souls, I lose my cool. And when they lie to the children, I can agree with the young rabbi that a millstone around their necks might be no bad thing. It's not that they are Christians—sometimes I'm a little bit Christian myself. It's that they aren't playing fair with the most important thing there is.

So an Omega Programme is not appealing? Of course not. We won't do that because of what I'll have to call a hunch. Hunch is a better word for many of us than faith, but it's really the same thing. We have a hunch about the ultimate "allrightness" of things. We have a hunch that, if there is a personal God, He wouldn't create people a certain way and then condemn them for being as they are. And if we don't think there's a personal God, we have the humility to recognise that we don't know everything yet; the jury's still out. We have a hunch that we shouldn't go around craning our necks skyward, but that we need to look for the truth where we find ourselves—in the world. And we have a hunch that, whether we've got it right or wrong, the sincerest gift that can be laid at the altar of truth is the honesty of our own hearts.

We shouldn't be too hard on the converts of the Alpha course, the Toronto blessings or any of these circuses. The way to be tolerant is to understand the ache of uncertainty that their misguided leaders, in their own ways, wish to heal. We can be tolerant of fundamentalists of whatever persuasion—Muslims, Hindus or Bible bashers—without yielding to their favourite pastime of condemnation. But I do think we need to oppose nonsense wherever it appears, and offer a way back to those who, in their emptiness, cannot separate the bath water from the baby.

It may be that we have a hunch that the adherents of certainty lack: an intuition that if there's a truth worth calling by that name, it will take care of itself without our campaigns and propaganda. Maybe we just trust that truth a little bit more. Maybe that's our gift: the blessing of uncertainty and the patience to live with it. And if it is, we need to share it around as best we can.

Transformation for Beginners

It's one of the oldest dreams of humanity. It's the substance of fairy tales like The Frog Prince—the source of those little adverts in the back of comic books and newspapers that promise to make you a karate expert or an internet millionaire, the thing that swells the numbers in further education colleges each September. It's the dream of the alchemist sweating over his oven, trying to turn lead into gold. It's the lure of the Christian fundamentalist who foresees leaping from a grave, shrugging off the corruption of the flesh, and being made whole and new at the sound of the Last Trump. It's something that affects each of us when we go on diets, start jogging or meditating, something that a lot of people talk about but few seem to accomplish. This dream is one of transformation.

Transformation is different from improvement. The idea of self-improvement is another constant of human life, probably the legacy of the restless Greek mind. The desire to be richer, smarter, prettier doesn't go away, and there are any number of ways you can try to fulfil this desire. But transformation isn't about any of these things. It's not concerned with personal advantage, but with personal awareness in the scheme, a sense of meshing with life in a new way.

The lure of transformation is seen everywhere. You can turn up your nose at ads promising hair re-growth or an MBA at home in your spare time, but it is harder to resist the lure of books and courses that promise to change your life by making you more spiritually aware, more conscious, more insightful. The welter of healing crystals and kundalini yoga, secrets of the pyramids and tree-hugging, attests to the persistence of an ancient hope: the transformation of the ordinary into something rare and beautiful.

Perhaps it's that we feel that life as we have conceived it for centuries has now reached a dead end. Maybe we feel that materialism, the endless pursuit of more convenience and less effort, has reached its limits. It could be that humanity is finally reaching the end of its long adolescence. It could be that there is a stirring in what C.G. Jung called the "collective unconscious" toward a new way of being and perceiving; a new yearning, if you will, for transformation.

The persistent image of transformation in the West has always been the figure of the alchemist. Alchemy was practised in medieval times before being banished from serious consideration by scientists. The alchemists were looking for ways not just to turn base metals into gold, but also to find a universal cure for all illness, to achieve immortality. The search for the Philosopher's Stone has been ridiculed for centuries now, ever since the rationalists of the Enlightenment pooh-poohed the ideas as childish dreams and turned themselves toward the more grownup preoccupations of a material universe. They preferred development to transformation, marvellous chemicals that fertilise fields that feed millions and poison rivers, machines that convey us in our millions while ruining the air, and a medical science that successfully targets pathogens but ignores the body's integrity. Good things along with bad, but unanimously dismissive of the alchemist's dream of turning the ordinary into the precious.

It was Carl Jung who in this century began to rummage about in this discarded metaphor for meaning. He was looking for models to use for his theory of human personality, and in the process he re-examined the ancient myths of the gods and other universal human symbols. As he began to re-open medieval texts that had been left on shelves as mere curios, Jung saw beneath the apparent to the meaning underneath, and resurrected the alchemist as a potent archetype, or pattern, of human striving for transformation.

Underlying the practice of alchemy was a root philosophy that was not unique to the medieval West. Its form could be glimpsed in many ancient traditions, as visible in the theology of the Egyptians as in the writings of Plato. This philosophy acknowledged the existence of a reality that underlies and permeates everything, and that is, largely invisible to humanity, but that persists in legend and myth and dream. It is the state of the Ideal according to Socrates, the breath of Vishnu to the Hindu, and it was known to Native Americans and inhabitants of ancient Zimbabwe as well. Seeing and experiencing this reality had been the preoccupation of mystics and shamans throughout history. In medieval alchemy, with its aim of transforming the ordinary into the precious, Jung recognized the symbols of the age-old search for the universal.

Whole new fields of psychotherapy have recently emerged within the tired old Freudian preoccupation with infantile sexuality, and depth psychology has re-opened the quest for the universal within the human psyche. These theories are mostly referred to as "transpersonal" precisely because they work from the idea that there is a point in the human mind that touches the universal, the collective unconscious of Jung and the Philosopher's Stone of the alchemist. In other words, explanations of human personality cannot be limited to, and thus transcend, the experiences of a single life—such as your having been dropped on your head by your mother at four months, say; they must be seen in a much larger and less verifiable context—the universal. And wellness is not limited to the cure of neurosis; it involves the opening of the connection to the eternal.

This vision of reality seems to be taking hold all around us. For me, it goes a long way to explaining what people do when they get together to engage in an act of worship. When you meditate or pray you are practising a form of personal alchemy, not reaching up for some gigantic celestial hand, but down, within, for the universal solvent that we feel underlies our pedestrian reality. We, like the alchemists, seem to know that the answer lies in some sort of process rather than in a theory or theology. We seem to know that there is a point inside everyone that touches the absolute, or eternal, or whatever you choose to call it.

I believe that the longing for personal transformation is a very deep one. It may wax and wane in the seasons of life as demands of the world affect us in different ways, but it is a human constant. It is often very visible in midlife, as the enthusiasm for mere getting and spending gets a little threadbare and we start to look again at parts of ourselves we have not explored. Transformation promises a deeper connection with the meaning hidden in the folds of the ordinary. It is both a goal and a path, a distant beacon and the journey toward it. It promises to take us out of the echo chamber of "how" into the depths of "why." As we mature spiritually we stop longing for magic charms and permanent catechisms; we begin to long for perception, to see through new eyes.

For those of you who thought this was a "how to" chapter—"Transformation in Ten Days without Dieting" or something like that—I have to disappoint you. I am still hunched over my alchemist's oven. If I crack the formula, I will let you know what it is right away, I promise. But I have a suspicion that each of us has got to find his or her own way. That's what the great sages seem to say, anyhow. But what I can offer are a couple of tips I have collected so far. You can decide if they are useful.

The first one comes from Paulo Coelho, the writer who has recently stood the dumbed-down publishing world on its head with a number of long parables. His book *The Alchemist* is of particular interest. It tells the story of a peasant boy in Spain, a shepherd, who, experiences a series of dreams and coincidences on a long journey in search of treasure. I won't spoil the book for you by recounting his picaresque travels through North Africa, but I will tell you that his goal is to reach the great pyramids of Egypt. Along the way, obsessed by his dream, events occur which beg whole new novels to be written, but he perseveres. When he finally reaches his goal, at the very edge of his strength and endurance, he dreams a profound dream of the very tree from beneath which he began in the first place. Beneath that tree he finds a treasure. The question is, "Was the journey necessary? Did he have to travel the whole Mediterranean world in order to find what he had already? Does this remind you of your own travel plans? I won't comment further, except perhaps to quote T.S. Eliot's "Little Gidding":

"We shall not cease from exploration, and the end of all our exploring will be to arrive where we started and know the place for the first time."

My second handy hint for personal transformation also comes—as so much of value does—from a dream. At a very important phase of my life, a time, you might say, that begged for transformation, I was depressed. Do you know what I mean by depression? Not just sadness, not just low energy levels, but a sense of bleak flatness that you would have to experience to understand. Life seemed to lose all its flavour, and I realised that I was treading a dangerous path near the dark forest of suicide and illness. Even this could not motivate me. If you've been there, you know what I mean.

And I had this dream. I seemed to be watching the news on television when a bulletin interrupted the regular programme. A clownlike figure in a top hat—sort of like a deranged Charlie Chaplin—appeared, pointing to a large white egg. In a mocking voice he said, "Terrible news, folks. The Corodin Egg is cracking!"

The dream woke me up in a sweat. I couldn't get it out of my mind. I took it to my friends, who looked up the word "corodin" in encyclopaedia and dictionary with no result. My therapist offered theories which didn't work. I had the disquieting feeling that I had received a message directly from my higher or deeper self, and that I was too thick to understand it. Some months later I was talking to a fellow student on a counselling course in one of those small groups you get put into and, without much enthusiasm, re-told the story of my dream. Wherever she is now—God bless her—I'll bet she's a damn good therapist, because she said, quietly, "The egg is corroding." Aha! The pure, smooth white egg of my youth was being destroyed. I was simultaneously relieved and terrified. At last I knew what was being said, but it was startling news.

I thought about it for a week. At the next class meeting, she came straight across the room to talk to me. She said that she had wanted to tell me about a question that had occurred to her after I told her the dream. What she said then has made a lot of difference to my life. It shows that gospel can come from any source at any time if we're alert, or—sometimes—even when we're not.

She said, "If the egg is cracking, I wonder what is being hatched." I knew then that my old ways of looking at things had suddenly evaporated. I had mourned the loss of a shell to the extent that I had ignored the most basic fundamental truth about an egg—it contains new life.

The alchemists had a term for the process of transforming something by fire. They called it "calcination"—literally, to reduce to bone, or calcium, the very most basic substance in the body. We might resist calcination—God knows I do—but sometimes it happens, and when it does, we need to be able to recognise the good in it. This is not easy, but will you believe me if I say it is necessary?

Do You Have the Right to be Happy?

A virtuous man searched all his life for happiness. After years of praying, an angel appeared one day at the foot of his prayer mat. "What is it you seek?" he said.

"I seek happiness," said the man.

"Come with me, then, and I'll show you where it might be found."

The angel took him instantly to a great palace. The palace was filled with beautiful things: paintings and sculptures, and a garden fragrant with exotic plants.

"Is it here?" asked the man. "Is this the place where happiness may be found?"

"It is," replied the angel.

The man immediately began to search all the rooms and corridors, picking up objects and carrying them to the angel. Each time he asked, "Is it this?" The angel said, "Not yet."

After hours of searching, the man grew tired. He had turned over hundreds of objects, but none of them were what he sought. As he rested, the beauty of the palace began to calm his spirit. He sat quietly and watched the play of light through the windows and the loveliness of the rooms. He had forgotten his search so thoroughly that when the angel appeared before him, the man was startled.

"This is it, isn't it?" the devout man said," This is happiness." The angel returned him to his prayer mat, knowing that the devout man had learned the hardest and most obvious lesson of all: happiness is found when you stop looking and start seeing.

Well, *do* you have the right to be happy?

However you may answer, it is interesting to note that only recently in human history would the question have very much meaning. Happiness in life throughout much of the past would have been the payoff for appeasing a wrathful and pernickety God or gods. The question of rights wouldn't have entered into it. It was a mystery whether or not you would live to be an old man or woman of thirty, or if God would strike you down with tooth abscesses or sabre-toothed tigers.

For many years happiness became a secondary concern for people. Firstly, when survival is an issue, happiness is a remote idea, except as it may be manifested in full bellies and relative safety from attack. As Abram Maslow pointed out with his famous pyramid, it's not likely you will be thinking about self-fulfilment if you're not getting enough to eat.

Secondly—at least in the West—theology was captured by a crowd of misery-gut dualists, who sold the idea that the phenomenal world was only a staging ground for heaven, where real happiness lay. This would be a heaven where you would be in even closer proximity to the judgmental God that you'd spent your life in fear of. I like the way Mark Twain dealt with it, saying that he had no interest in being surrounded by goody-goodies for eternity; he reckoned all the best parties would be in Hell.

In any event, the world was no place to find happiness. Holiness, yes. Honour, possibly. But happiness was reserved until the afterlife of the lucky and diligent few who bent their backs and cowered before God. Are we surprised that a gang of Enlightenment upstarts came up with a document actually describing the "pursuit of happiness" as a basic human right? When the writers of the American Declaration of Independence saw fit to overthrow the divine right of kings and the idea of unquestioning submission to worldly authority, they also made a rallying cry of what had until shortly before then been a mad idea—the right of people to happiness in this world.

What the early Enlightenment claimants to happiness were probably referring to was material happiness: a good living would have been almost a synonym. A warm safe bed and enough to eat already exceeded the expectations of all the centuries past; more refined notions of spiritual satisfaction were the obsessions of poets and the idle rich. But as the possibility of material well-being grew through the nineteenth century, ideas of happiness of a more absolute sort appeared. Poets such as Blake and Wordsworth in England sounded a warning that mere materialism wasn't going to result in the attainment of happiness, after all. Fulfilment did lie in this world, but not through the accretion of wealth. It had more to do with a process of self-cultivation, an idea originally foreseen by the precocious Greeks.

Thus began a time of seeking for fulfilment that today has become a major obsession. The post-modernist philosopher Michel Foucault termed the self-help and human potential movement "technologies of the self." That is, a series of processes enacted by the person upon the person with the aim of some kind of transformation. In other words, a version of the pursuit of happiness. The examples are legion: *How to Win Friends and Influence People*, Reiki, macrobiotic diet, primal scream therapy, neuro-linguistic programming, astrology, orgone boxes, re-birthing, Rolfing, the inneagram, ginseng, automatic writing, crystal healing, LSD. Have I forgotten a few? Numerology, spiritual autobiography, kundalini yoga, sweat lodges, Iron John, circle dancing, reflexology, Bach flower remedies, tree hugging, sensory deprivation, ley line walking, aromatherapy. I'm getting tired. There are probably a thousand others I could mention that will be touted at the next Body, Mind and Spirit Fair near you.

I'm not knocking any of these activities; I practice some of them myself. The point is that we have become increasingly preoccupied with the pursuit of elusive happiness. We feel that there must be some ancient trick or some arduous procedure that will open the gates for us and make us happy. More, we may have begun to feel a little desperate; the right to happiness is beginning to look like the *duty* to be happy. It is not cool to display emptiness and to be unhappy. All the best people are getting their acts together, and if they're not, they're victims of a trendy sort. The inner child is wounded, perhaps, or the patriarchal structure has banished the feminine from their lives. The dark night of the soul has become popular. By its other name—clinical depression—it has become a growth industry. If we take Prozac, we do it in secret. Anyway, it's our right to be happy, isn't it? Or is it our duty?

So it is interesting that whereas once people conceived of attaining happiness simply as a matter of getting more and more stuff, there is a recent trend that focuses on transformation. Not that materialism has suffered much. Getting and spending is still enjoying mass popularity. But there are a growing number of us that feel happiness needs to be sought through changing ourselves in some way. Maybe because our parents didn't do something well in our infancy. Maybe because capitalism degrades, or because the Druids are gone. Maybe it's because we have a block in our *chi*, or aren't *feng shui* enough. Whatever the reason, there is something that needs changing, healing, transforming.

Happiness still seems to elude us. The hurrier we chase it, the behinder we get. Could it be that this is because—not only do we not know what we want—we wouldn't recognise it if it bit us on the ankle? How many times have we said, "That was probably the happiest time of my life," meaning perhaps, that we didn't know it at the time. Maybe we don't know what happiness is like. Maybe we should take some advice from a few old-fashioned experts.

Plato, who is sometimes blamed for creating the dualism that made heaven heavenly and the world drab, has probably had a bum rap from history. Unlike the Stoics and other pre-Socratic lifestyles, Plato and his teacher Socrates seem to have had a fair idea about earthly happiness. In one discourse, Plato talks about the difference between pleasure and happiness. This is known as the "argument of the leaky jug." A Hedonist tried to claim that happiness is found in the accumulation of pleasure and the avoidance of pain. He said that life is like a jug with a hole in it. The water you pour in is pleasure; the water that leaks out is pain. The trick is to pour in more pleasure than you experience pain. That's the way to be happy.

Plato took him gently through a series of Socratic questions that differentiate pleasure from happiness. His point is that happiness has more to do with a relationship to the Real than to the distraction of the senses. In other words, happiness is not created but *found*. When something is found, it cannot be non-existent; it must have been there all along, lying just out of sight.

This concept of *found happiness* was shared by the Buddha. He would have made short work of the Hedonist, too. In contrast to seeking pleasure and avoiding pain, Gautama pointed out that they were the same thing, and that liberation lies in transcending both. The source of true happiness lies in seeing through the false opposites of pain and pleasure, good and evil, once again to the Real. In Buddhism this would mean Nirvana, or liberation from the wheel of opposites, cause and effect.

The rabbi Jesus took it even further. His sermons were full of paradox: gaining one's life is losing it; living is found through dying, and other brain teasers. He made a point of saying that seeking wealth—trying to stave off suffering through accumulation—came at the cost of one's soul. This was more than the hair-shirt masochism of certain religious orders, because all the evidence points to a rather merry Jesus who enjoyed good wine and interesting companions. And happiness did not just lie in the sweet by-and-by of some of his more life-hating subsequent followers: the Kingdom of Heaven was "at hand", right here and now, if only we could be bothered to see it.

The teacher Meher Baba used to frustrate the seekers that gathered around him. For one thing, he didn't speak for the more than forty years that preceded his death. He indicated that there had been plenty of words spoken throughout history to very little real effect. He gave few orders and advocated little technique in the spiritual search. He offered general advice to all seekers of truth, however. He said, "Don't worry. Be happy." He said that long before the Reggae song, by the way. Once, when someone seemed to take the phrase lightly, Baba gestured sternly that the order was serious. To worry was to underestimate God, and to be happy was the most sincere way to pray.

There's something there that has always intrigued me. The statement says that the opposite of happiness is worry. Worry is that famous thing that does no good, changes nothing. Its opposite, being happy despite everything, seems to be at the very heart of what we call worship. It is, indeed, a way of putting oneself in touch with the Real, even though you can't see it. It is faith on wheels. Meher Baba said it opened a person up to the presence of God. It is also the greatest gift I can think of, not just for yourself, but for your companions.

But being asked to be happy without any good reason is a tough one, isn't it? On the face of it, it seems—if not impossible—a little mindless. It's like being asked to leapfrog over yourself, and wind up at your destination before you make your journey. A Zen master was once asked what enlightenment was like. He answered, "Before enlightenment, I chopped wood and carried water. After enlightenment, I chop wood and carry water." This may mean that the journey to happiness really has the starting point as its destination.

Since happiness is not made, but found, the question becomes, "Where do we find it?" And the answer, given thousands of times, over and over by the great voices of every generation seems to say "It's right here. Just open your eyes and see." Happiness is not just your birthright; it is who you really are. Don't worry. Be happy. Just do it. And if you manage it, for God's sake show the rest of us how.

Hunting for Unicorns

One day in 1932, a motorist was driving alongside a large lake in Scotland. From his car window he saw—or so he reported—an odd creature swimming above the waves. The creature was large, so large that its body was composed of two huge humps, like a snake's, and a head riding high, yards above the surface. This was the debut of a favourite modern legend, the Loch Ness monster.

I'm told that on a good day at Loch Ness there can be hundreds of people with field glasses trained on the water. There have been several other sightings over the years, and even a few grainy photographic attempts at proof. At least one scientific expedition has used sonar and underwater photography to attempt to debunk the monster's existence, with indifferent results. People seem determined to believe that "Nessie" exists. Most of these are probably relatively sensible people, not given to fanciful ideas or weird theories. Some may even be scientists or from other jobs that require the use of reason as a guide. They have found in this modern day miracle a way of believing the unlikely, or even the impossible.

In Europe, in the Middle Ages, people were obsessed with the unicorn, a beast with the breast of a lion, the legs of a deer and a single spiralled horn growing from its forehead. It was rumoured to be the only creature that could kill an elephant, which in those days before world travel must have seemed an equally mysterious creature. So great was the unicorn's fascination for people that not only did it appear on tapestries and banners—such as the heraldic seal of Scotland—but pilgrims actually went in search of it in forests. The divines of the era equated it, naturally, with Jesus Christ. And without apparent irony, it was thought to be found only in the presence of virgins, presumably another rarity.

The unicorn has gone. Some TV naturalist would have told us if they still existed, wouldn't they? There would have been a programme on prime time viewing. There are thousands of marvellous things out there in the forests and seas of the world: giant manta rays, flying mammals, and even glowing things at the high-pressure bottoms of seas, but not a mermaid or a unicorn in sight. It's possible to say that the jury is still out on the Loch Ness Monster, but it's not looking good so far.

What interests me about all this is not whether Nessie exists, or whether the aliens of the *X-Files* have actually kidnapped people, but why the belief persists at all. What have these fantastical experiences of the extraordinary got to tell us about ourselves and the way we view the world? How is it that otherwise sensible people can sit freezing on the shores of a Scottish lake hoping for a glimpse of the impossible?

Those of you that have children of a certain age are about to see the sad exit of Father Christmas from the scene. No more careful concealment of boxes, no more tiptoeing around after making sure the kids are asleep. And no more of that irrational joy as the children confront the supernatural at six a.m. on the 25th of December. From now on, gifts will be given, pleasure savoured, turkey eaten, but that almost sacred sense of something extraordinary having manifested in the ordinariness of your living room will be missing. Reason, that old gangster, will rule OK.

We are protective about myths. We don't want older siblings blowing Santa's cover prematurely, though, odds are, they will. Most of us feel a little deflated when a myth is debunked. When they carbon-dated the Shroud of Turin and found it to be a much younger cloth than Jesus could have been wrapped in, I—no Christian, certainly no Catholic—felt robbed. I wanted the cloth to be real. Even when Yuri Geller's magic spoons are bent equally well by a stage magician in Blackpool, I'm annoyed. It seems that I need some token of the miraculous in my life. More than that, I want there to be things that scientists can't explain away with their totalitarian logic. There has to be some token among the all-too-explainable events of life of the magical and transcendent. Without even the odd bent spoon or flying saucer, how can I believe in something like God?

Any good philosopher will be scowling at me right now. That's because he or she knows that it isn't really reason that's the gangster of the piece, but the uses to which we want to put it. We want the miraculous to exist despite the hunger for explanation we are so proud of, and the two needs don't work harmoniously alongside each other. When a sunset reveals itself to be light refracted by dust motes in the atmosphere, we win knowledge and lose wonder. When the turning of a sunflower toward the sun is explained away as the thermally determined swelling and contracting of cells instead of a form of worship, we put this in our biology notebooks and feel cheated. When they finally get around to analysing the genetic traces of saints and mystics and finding enhanced levels of serotonin in the brain cells, it is possible that Rumi and Teresa of Avila will stop selling books. Our need for explanation will have finally eaten us alive.

What we are looking for in Loch Ness and on the *X-Files* reruns isn't consistent with explanation. What we are looking for is an entirely separate way of understanding the world that has little or nothing to do with proof. The Rabbi Jesus was demonstrably angry when his disciples asked for proof of his divinity. He called them a "generation of vipers, who demand a sign." Meher Baba put it another way in the words of the title: "Asking to understand God is like asking to see with your ears." It seems that there is another form of knowing that has nothing to do with proof or scientific observation. It has more to do with Paul's idea of faith—the "evidence of things unseen."

We wander around in the world believing what we see. "Show me" we say, and feel a bitter pleasure in pooh-poohing the wondrous. But a certain reluctance—call it nostalgia—afflicts us. There must be more than this mere cataloguing of events, weighing and measuring of things. The bank manager who can apply ruthless logic to your account details reads the horoscope page in the newspaper at lunchtime.

The cynical cocaine dealer makes sure his flat is *feng shui*. And I know a doctor who eats her apple seeds, despite the debunking of amygdaline as a cancer cure-all. The remnants of belief in the miraculous survive even into this age of scientific answers, even though they may be squeezed uncomfortably into superstitious games.

I see all these unicorn theories as being lovely scented handkerchiefs dropped by someone or something we might as well call God. Because I see that there is a quality in human beings that makes them vulnerable to unreason, I want to start looking there for the way to real understanding. I want to see the persistence of hope as a sign that, despite the straitjacket of our limited knowledge, there is reason to trust in the miraculous after all.

Most of what we say about God, the universe and all that uses the third person singular. When we talk about God, if we do at all, it is largely in terms of "He", "She" or "It." In other words, we spend most of our time theorising and explaining. This is the shoddy home of the limited ego, still trying to make explanations and find proof.

But there is a different way to go about it. Martin Buber, the Jewish theologian, wrote a seminal book entitled *I, Thou*. He said that in most of our dealings with others, we take a stand described as "I, it." That is, we objectify, make objects out of, others. The "I" is a subject, experienced subjectively, and the other person is an object, something we observe, theorise about and limit to the extent of our own understanding. He said that we need to move from "I, it" to "I, thou," to make a second subject of the other, and by so doing to break the hegemony of the little self that is the claimant to being the centre of the universe.

Without being too abstract about this, you might say that when you engage in dialogue with someone else, you make them real to you. Also, conversation breaks the barrier of projection you have placed upon them through your own theories and prejudices. You move from a position of mere explanation and description to one of experience of another's reality. This is sometimes practiced in workshops. Sometimes it is done spontaneously with a lover or friend. It is rare, but when it happens, the universe seems to expand, attitudes melt and for a while the tyranny of the little ego is broken.

Conversations between prison camp guards and prisoners are usually wisely forbidden. This is because the prisoner might become a subject rather than an object, bringing chaos to the project of domination and control. The "explanation" of someone as merely a Jew or communist yields to the experience of the other as a subject, like yourself. In other words, "I, thou." When the "I" meets the "thou," ethnic cleansing and similar horrors become less possible. The "it," the result of mere explanation, yields to the "thou," where the possibility of love and understanding lives.

Buber wasn't just talking about relationships between people. He also meant an approach to that most mysterious relationship of all, between people and God. I don't mean to bore you with my usual explanation of what I mean by this contentious little three-letter word. It's perfectly all right with me if you want to use your own synonym: "spirit of meaning," "ground of being," "universe," etc. But I am referring to something both greater and more inclusive then ourselves. And, yes, I am talking about someone or something that can be addressed, not just talked about. Besides, it's easy to spell.

Theologians talk about God. That's what the word means: "God talk." But the other group whose words we so often listen to here—the mystics of every tradition—talk *to* God. In other words, they raise the stakes of the game by moving the subject from the third person singular to the second person singular: "I, thou." Having explanations, even convincing ones delivered by inspiring preachers, keeps God in the category of object. Talking *to* God, whoever or whatever your idea of that being might be, makes a subject out of mere description. A conversation becomes possible.

Those of us who want to believe in unicorns, who have a unicorn-shaped hole in their heads, have only got one choice: go out there into the forest and look for one. Those of us, who, finding explanations poor fare for our soul's hunger, need to seek an encounter. Yes, even those of us who can't or won't believe in God need to put their money where their secret heart is and go looking for the real.

The Hindu saying, "The sandalwood always smells sweet whether you are there or not" means that the fragrance of reality cannot be apprehended by speculation, much less by denial. To smell the sandalwood you have to open the box where it is kept whether you believe that there is anything inside or not. That's the key to finding what you need.

Those who are certain there can be no God have my sympathy. I share their doubts and fear of getting it wrong. But to them, I would say, "What, really, have you got to lose?" If you risk getting wet and cold in some forest only to find that there are no unicorns, isn't that better than merely bragging that you already know? And to those who can't pray because they feel there's no one on the other end of the line, I would say, isn't it worth a try? Have you ever really tried? Come on, now—*really*?

If you want to know about God, don't ask me. Ask Him.

Keeping up Appearances

One of my heroes was a con man.

The great impresario P.T. Barnum may have been a trickster, but there was more to him, just as there is to all of us. With his belief-defying acts of fakery—such things as the so-called Cardiff Giant and the mummy of a mermaid—he was exhibiting a precocious grasp of the fledgling science of psychology. His success depended upon his awareness of one central fact of human nature: humans enjoy being fooled. The illusion is a precious possession of ours. Let an expedition scour Loch Ness and prove beyond doubt that there is no Nessie the friendly monster. What would ensue is a mass cry of outrage. We want there to be harmless dragons. Let carbon dating and DNA sampling disprove the Shroud of Turin as the winding sheet of Jesus; are we pleased? No, in time the same ingenuity of mind that debunks myth will find a fresh way to believe in it again, and—as has currently happened—the whole longed-for mystery of the Shroud can be re-opened with the blessing of the Pope. We have a strong appetite for playing the fool.

Carl Jung, with his deft hand in working at the margins of myth and reality, once spoke about the existence of flying saucers. He pointed out that people needed to believe in them because, in their hearts, they wanted to fly "east of the Sun and west of the Moon." The sightings of UFO's were reflections of the collective unconscious desire to penetrate the surface of mere reality in search of meaning. In other words, we humans intuit that there is more to reality than just the surface that can be weighed, described and measured. But debarred since childhood from the comfort of fairy tales, our minds almost involuntarily seek other avenues of escape from the dull stasis of pedestrian life.

Just outside our range of vision, fleeing as we turn our heads, lying doggo beneath the most ordinary, it seems, there is an opening to the wonderful. This idea strikes a chord in us; it can only be relegated to the dusty chest of childish fantasy by the hardest of cynics. It almost seems as if we know that hidden in the frog of daily life there is a prince, and a glimpse of the eternal.

We may know this from the teachings of Hinduism, which tell us that everything we perceive is a great illusion, like a mega-presentation of P.T. Barnum, the dance of the God, Maya. Or from Plato, whose solitary man escaped from the flickering shadow images of the cave and went out into the unbearable brightness of reality. Or even from physicists following Einstein, who have their own ways of revealing that beyond the limits of scientific descriptions lies a universal mind that swirls the stardust in patterns that we only interpret, but cannot truly understand.

When we were children we knew that reality had holes in it. We loved stories of fairies and magic carpets and princesses in towers. We didn't have to account for their veracity; we just enjoyed them. We were probably indulged in this by doting parents and grandparents who knew unconsciously that we were the very important couriers of the improbable for the whole of our culture. By reading fairy tales and worthy juvenile best-sellers to our own children, we are voyeuristically re-entering the world from which we were so cruelly banished by adulthood. We are re-visiting the part of ourselves that may well be wiser than our cultivated rationality, the part from which springs not just poetry, but mystical experience as well. This childish art of seeing through, or beyond, reality may be limited, but has not been destroyed; it is alive in our children. I think that's why Jesus annoyed everyone by telling them that they had to become like little children. He could have been saying not, "Grow up," but, "Grow down."

But at a certain point we all begin to lose easy access to the hidden miraculous. The princesses and magic castles become mere nonsense. Even though voices such as that of Jung warn us that the castles were just rude glimpses of something actual, symbols of a world that in many ways is more "real" than the one we occupy, we plug our ears and grow up. Those of us who don't may find ourselves marginalised, banished to Bohemian colonies or even institutions. This is not just because society wills it to be so; it is to a great degree self-enforcing. Because, at a certain point, we see that all is not happy endings and golden eggs, but is also frightening, with witches and monsters and—yes—death, too.

When this happens, we metaphorically leave the enchanted wood and come back to the hearth fire. We seek comfort in the ordinary, alongside our parents. We want explanations, not miracles. In psychological terms, we allow our sense of self to reside in the narrow confines of the ego and we banish everything else into the unconscious. In a very real sense, we become co-conspirators in a safe and shallow game. We cultivate the surfaces and ignore the depths. But we also begin to cling to a new kind of illusion, to keep up the appearances at the cost of the real. So what if there's no God we can spend whole afternoons talking to in the wood? At least there's no Devil to haul us into the pit. So what if the soul isn't eternal? We've got antibiotics and genetic therapy to keep us safe. These new illusions are not just less comforting; they are much less fun.

Once installed in the new narrow field of agreed illusion, we belong. And something more: each of us becomes a kind of reality cop, editing and re-enforcing the appearances we have agreed upon. Even the best of us dislikes it when the appearances are challenged. Social custom reflects and supervises the agreed party line: adulterers are stoned, strangers are isolated, widows left to starve. Or, today, people who "see things" are institutionalised or become homeless under the arches. Experimentation with mind—altering substances is made illegal; artists are more indulged than admired.

The pattern filters down into all our relationships. There are couples who co-conspire in a pact to avoid mutual challenge and simply collect anniversaries. They agree to stay together despite their individual needs to grow and change. They agree to share in a common act of appearances, and after a while it doesn't seem to hurt any more. People opt for conservatism as a life strategy, holding hard to a tightrope walk, daring to look neither right nor left, for fear of being overwhelmed by either light or darkness.

Groups do the same thing. Village peasants, economic classes, even nation states. Yes, churches, too. They hang together in a mutually agreed fashion based on their need for safety. Not just the safety from physical terrors, but from the myth-destroying influence of the new. The phrase "We have always done things like this," hides the reluctance to see things as they are. If things change, there is a risk that the woolly blanket of their shared conspiracy will be ripped away.

What lies behind all this is fear. The first glimpse of the witch in the wardrobe sends warning signals to the child. And at the point when accepting the universe in both its kindly and fearsome aspects is presented, most of us shrink back. Even though we may suspect that appearances are only that, we still prefer them to the wild trip into the unknown. A little like that lovely club, the Flat Earth Society, we brandish a motto which says, "Beyond this place be monsters."

What, then, is the motive for pretending to be richer, smarter, better than others? Why do we insist upon things being fixed, the way they always were? Why do we want others to conform, and react with anger when they do not? How can we not bore ourselves with playing the fool? The answer is not all that complicated: whatever breaks the spell of common pretence creates fear.

Poets and mystics have often told us that "love casts out fear," another way of saying that the opposite of love is not hate, but fear. If love is the force in the universe that unites and pulls things together, from gravity, to animal attraction, to the apotheosis of saints, then fear is the opposite force that repels, isolates and makes static. We are endowed with both qualities, for however hardened we may become to what lies outside our pedestrian word view, love finds ways to leak in, to erase the appearances. An eye that twinkles at the precisely right moment, sending thrills of romantic energy down to your marrow, the small, sticky hand of a grandchild in your own, the bubbling up of cosmic humour at a moment so absurd that the mantle of illusion is slightly parted—all these aspects of love stalk us, beset us, live in us. A favourite hymn line of mine used to be "O Love That Will Not Let Me Go," meaning just this to me. Love is too strong to be banished altogether. Like fear, it will not let us go, not while we live.

Love, said Paul, the P.T. Barnum of the early church, is neither proud nor puffed up. I might add that love takes no prisoners; it is ruthless with any form of pretence. The object of love demands to be known, to be seen at the closest of ranges, and to be accepted, no matter what. If you love someone—that is, if you have passed beyond the shallow stages of lust and infatuation—you love them in their uniqueness, no matter how broken or imperfect. The warts and all are not something to be overlooked, through a cosmetic contract of pretence, but to be held as the very tokens of individuality.

And love won't stop there. It just goes on spreading, changing everything it touches. It becomes a lens through which one can view creation with new eyes. In the great Eastern tale of Majnu and Layla, the human love that drove them on a search for each other brought them both to the threshold of God. I believe that the universal spirit is opportunistic; it will use the love you have in whatever form to bring you back to itself. It is, after all, only fear that gets in the way.

Love has a lot of faces. Sometimes it appears as an enemy, something that wants to bedevil you in the comfy nest of appearances you have built for yourself. You may wish to shoo it away, saying, "I'm all right, Jack," and roll over and go back to sleep. But, springing as it does from the deep kind heart of the universe, it's too strong for that—"so high you can't get over it, so low you can't get under it...." The poet Francis Thompson described it as a "hound of heaven" that "chased him down all the nights and all the days..." Usually, in one way or another, love hurts as it heals, because having bandages ripped away is always painful.

So there is bad news and good news for all of us. The bad news is that we shall be stripped of our illusions, no matter how tightly we hold on to them, and be lovingly turned toward the dark wood we have so carefully learned to avoid. The good news is simply this: the loving face of the universe will be there to meet us when we have had done with our ruses and tricks and dared to look unblinking into the unknown.

Staying Alive

Did you practice magic rituals as a child? I did. Things like making incantations when my friends and I buried a dead seagull. Things like not stepping on cracks in the sidewalk in case—as the little rhyme went—I would "break my mother's back." I had to be home by six o'clock for supper, but even when I was running late, I dragged a bamboo cane from Jimmy Jowers' hedge over every picket fence on my block.

Looking back now, I can give all sorts of interpretations to those rituals. They were what are called "superstitions." "A belief or practice resulting from ignorance, or fear of the unknown.... A belief maintained despite evidence to the contrary," according to my dictionary. They certainly qualified on these two counts. Children are naive—nearly everything is unknown. The word *superstition* is derived from Latin meaning "to stand over, as witness, victor or survivor." By doing these magic rituals one could "stand over" the fearsome and irrational nature of events, and endow them with at least some sort of meaning.

Anthropologists have long associated the universal existence of religion with just this sort of superstitious behaviour. If crops failed, that must be because there hadn't been sufficient sacrifice made last harvest. If your enemies drove you away from a choice hunting spot, that was because there were too many or too few sets of twins in your ranks, or because the tribe had allowed left-handed children to live. Rituals arose in this fertile seedbed of ignorance and fear. Rituals begin as appeasement or correct etiquette toward the unknown forces. They are part of the magic that keeps you safe.

The thing about ritual is that it becomes automatic. It begins to take on a life of its own, whether or not it was originally based on some rough logic. Like the guru who tied up a hyperactive cat during meditation, and whose disciples subsequently tied up a token cat for centuries, even eventually making holy statues of a cat with a string round its neck. When I carefully avoided the seams in the pavement as a child, I was joining my ancestors in appeasing the gods and obeying the folk wisdom of my peers. My compliance was more or less unquestioning. If you ask a nine-year-old if he really believes that an incautious footstep in the wrong place has a direct relationship with the health of his mother's vertebrae, he'll probably just shrug. Shrug, and go on stepping carefully over the cracks. Even at that age he knows that adult ideas only work for adults, and that there are things never dreamed of in Horatio's philosophy.

Many rituals stay with us throughout life. We can be as rational as you please, but how many of us can raise our right hand and testify that our lives are free of superstitious ritual? What's your response to spilt salt, a solitary magpie, a ladder in your path? Even if none of these things affect you, think about this: I started asking the couples I was marrying over the last few years if they had seen each other before the ceremony on the day. None had, even the great majority who were already living together. And most brides have carefully garnered something old, something new, something borrowed and something blue. It's a fact. When the minister asks, there is often a slightly guilty head ducking with the reply, as if they feel embarrassed about dealing with gods older than those in the church.

The superstitious remedies may change over time, but the irrational fear of the unknown never really leaves us. Our rationalist background has historically defied many sorts of superstition and done battle against ignorance. We are proud of that. But take a little ride with me to some of your local churches, and you'll find that the snake of superstition may have been scotched but not killed. As M. Scott Peck has said, churches are full of people who swear they'll leave if you move the communion rail four inches (and others who'll leave if you don't). I used to preach in churches where a lit chalice wasn't used, because you could only light candles during Advent. This was more than custom; it was superstition. In matters of the unknown, the old gods are still around.

Ritual, of course, is not always a bad thing. It could wear the definition usually applied to a sacrament: "a visible, outward sign of an invisible, inner reality." Some rituals cement a community together in a positive way. In fact, some people lucidly suggest that we are starved for creative ritual. They propose various rites to solve this, but find that they don't often work. Rituals *emerge;* they are not created from the left brain, but from some older, more intuitive place in us.

What about our own personal rituals? Do you do things a certain way every morning? Are you frustrated when the pattern is interrupted? I have several inviolable rituals. I take half an aspirin every morning, a little magic bullet to protect myself against heart attack. Never mind that I have fallen prey to smoking, cholesterol over-indulgences, too little exercise and so on. When I'm away on a weekend conference and find I've left my little white pills behind, I feel very uneasy. This is not a medical thing; it is magic. My ritual is actually superstitious. It's about dealing with the imponderables of a still unknown universe. It's about staying alive.

I think that if we were able to take a clear and unbiased look at our lives we would find that "staying alive" explains a lot of the mysteries of our behaviour. I didn't say *living*, I said *staying alive*, which is a little different. *Staying* is from the same linguistic root we saw in *superstition*, meaning standing. A close cousin is *stasis*: "a state of static balance or equilibrium; stagnation." We see our lives as needing to be constantly guarded, eked out with the greatest care, defended against that ultimate disaster—becoming dead.

Our strategies include ritual, but that's not the only way we have of avoiding death. I know someone who has recently suffered from a heart problem. He has spent months of concentrated effort in using the internet for genealogical research of his family. However interesting this may be, I can't help feeling that in his case it's really about magic, using the centuries of life past as a talisman against the shadow of death in the present.

We can name a dozen more false strategies to avoid death. A mother unable to let her grown children fly from the nest, because they carry her best hope of immortality. An artist driven by the need for fame, so that at least his name outlives his flesh. A pair of exercise junkies recently returned from the park, red faced and limping, having outrun the Grim Reaper once again. A dieter living on juice from fresh organic vegetables and starting to look a little pale. Someone with a red-veined nose who has been seeking the eternal spirit in the infernal spirits of the bottle. Even going to church can be a kind of bargain with God; we accumulate gold stars on our cards to dazzle the Devil. The list is endless because every one of us has some secret charm to ward off the end, even if we aren't aware of it.

If superstition is the seedbed of religion as the academics say, we can understand why we do church things in certain ways. The word *worship*, at last coming under attack from some of our best thinkers, holds this image for me. I can find little difference between the priest handing out blessings and charms according to traditional church liturgy and the boy avoiding cracks. God is unknown and dangerous. Despite the reassurance the Presbyterians gave me about the loving Father, I could never quite square it with the dire expression "fear of the Lord." Sometimes I felt as if there was someone—I'll call him "Butch"—who needed a weekly dose of propitiation and flattery. Remember the old lines from the Anglican Communion service? "Lord, we are not worthy to eat the crumbs that fall from your table..." and a lot more grovelling besides. This "Butch" may have been mercifully supposed dead in 1966, but the god he had taken the place of, the old god that demanded your firstborn, made you sacrifice your best ewe, who could be warded off or made docile by a few choice incantations—that god is alive and well and hiding in the childhood wardrobe of our minds, right next to the witch.

Thankfully, there have been other voices, if you know how to listen to them. They are clear and calm and strangely attractive despite, or perhaps because of, their use of paradox. Like the voice of Jesus, reminding us to have no care for the morrow. Like the Buddha, sitting under the Bo tree at the end of the world, waving us all through toward non-existence, and smiling. Like Rumi, who asks us to be done with the foolishness of staying alive, who speaks to us from awareness that life is a tool more than a treasure. Like those of us who direct our gaze toward a world where life is *spent*, not hoarded, those who realise that merely staying alive is something even a cockroach comprehends, but that living, real living, is something utterly different Living is merging with life, becoming life, touching that disputed point that Jesus called eternal, not staking oneself down to the fleeting and impermanent.

Recently certain scientists have been talking about a growing trend to take risks. It seems that our modern drive to make life sterilised, homogenised and odour-free has stirred atavistic reactions in us. People are sky diving, rock climbing, paragliding. They indulge in risky sex and drugs and gamble as day traders on the stock exchanges. Even American cabinet members have been seen bungee jumping into deep gorges. The scientists have concluded that this risky behaviour is a re-assertion of something essential in humanity, something that enabled prehistoric man to win through in an evolutionary world of growth and challenge, something as necessary to survival as the longing for safety. Taking Abram Maslow's revered pyramid of human needs, with safety at its foundation, and turning it on its head, they express concern that if these urges to take risks do not find harmless outlets they may make us do mad things, like start wars. In short, we are being told that human beings actually need to take risks, to break out of carefully constructed safety into the dangers of a more primitive world.

A new form of sport has come into being. It is called extreme sport, because it involves doing extreme things. Like cycling off a mountain, or climbing up one without ropes and pitons. Like scaling a skyscraper with your fingernails, or midnight roller-blading on the Paris ring road.

When practitioners of extreme sport are interviewed, they are hard pressed to explain the attraction. One thing they often say is that it makes them feel more alive. This is a paradox, isn't it? How can you bat your eyelashes at death and be closer to life? We can dismiss them as cranks, if we wish. After all, people have gone over Niagara Falls in barrels before. But the trend is undeniably growing: courting death to find life.

I think the urge to risk physical death may really be a signal for something spiritual. The place for all that misplaced bravura is not a bridge or a mountain; it's the soul. I mean the kind of extreme sport urged by Rumi. Someone I know calls it "pickaxe theology." Don't get too used to the house you live in, he says. You're just a temporary tenant. Listen to him: tear down this house! Stop sewing small patches on torn clothing. Come out into the arena where superstition and personal magic can't exist. Where staying alive is not a futile, meaningless pursuit. Your tenancy in this impermanent house is about something. Now is the time to find the treasure buried in the foundations.

This call is tantalising, but it means taking big risks. It means abandoning the safe corners where you've been hiding. It means standing on the edge and shouting and laughing with God. It overturns all the formulae, just like Jesus did when he said: "He who would gain his life shall lose it." Or Meher Baba: "Real being is dying through loving." Those voices are urging you not to mountain climbing, but to an even riskier kind of risk. They are inviting you to lose the superstitious magic of your safe ways and to rely only on the promise found written in your soul. They are saying: trust God, risk living fully, rejoice. You cannot save your life. You *are* life, and there is just one way to discover that. Creep up to the cliff edge of real living, which can be found every day in a million ways. Creep up there, stand shoulder to shoulder with those other heroes. Take a deep breath, forget all those magic formulae, and jump.

Geronimo!

Learning from the Losers

"What would you do if I sang out of tune? Would you stand up and walk out on me?" Remember those words to the Beatles song? That might be the anthem of most ministers I know. They are singing it unconsciously as they climb up into their pulpits to offer what small pearls of wisdom they may have found in the past week. Sometimes they joke about it: "You're only as good as your last sermon," they say.

We know that's ridiculous. Well, it is, isn't it? Because nobody is so wise that the pearls come easily. Nobody is so eloquent that they can't trip over their tongues and talk nonsense. Nobody has such perfect pitch that they don't sometimes sing a little flat. Come to think of it, nobody is so good with numbers that they don't make mistakes. Nobody is such a good manager that they don't overlook important things. Everybody, from the cleaners at the airport to cabinet ministers, gets it wrong sometimes.

Then why are we so guarded about our small failures and lack of ability? Why is the fear of failure the main thing that sends people to the chemist for tranquillizers and turns families to war zones around the time of school exams? And at its most macabre limits, why does Japan have dozens of what are called "infant suicides" every year at the time of competitive examinations for good school places? What is it about failure that so terrifies us in ourselves and makes such good reading when it happens to somebody important?

No one wants to be a loser. We may approve of competition, extol the virtues—with good reason—of the competitive marketplace as a provider of wealth—spend a great deal of our time watching athletes run faster, jump higher and catch more balls, but we avoid thinking about running slower, jumping not so high—losing, in short. Even if we aren't high flyers, we may lose sleep over someone preferring a neighbour's scones to our own, or someone else's slightly more beautiful grandchild. If we were able to write the script of our lives—as so many of us foolishly believe we do—we would always win. We'd be magnanimous in victory, charming and generous with the losers, but still winners.

It's a cliché but it's true: the first thing people want to know about you after they learn your name is what you do for a living. He's "something in the City," she's a deputy head teacher, little Nigel won first place in the butterfly stroke in his division. This confusion of what we do with who we are is natural in a competitive environment, but it's misleading. Where are the ones who aren't something in the City—who are unemployed following a nervous breakdown? The ones who failed their exams and never went to college, the child who isn't good at sports or studies, either? We know they're around; our winning is dependent, after all, on their losing out. With all these winners about, who will teach us how to be a good loser?

The best-known loser in history, of course, was Jesus of Nazareth. After disappointing his mother and refusing the honest trade of his father, young Jesus became an itinerant preacher, sleeping rough with a few lower class mates and never doing a lick of honest work. Not only did he keep the company of losers—a prostitute, a publican, a despised tax collector, to name a few—he even preached about "the least of these" and said that coming in last was a good thing. He proved it by being sold out by his best friends and dying an ignominious death between two common criminals. What had happened to all that promise shown by the twelve-year-old whiz kid at the temple? All that ability with words, turning the questions of the Pharisees inside out, the knack of drawing big crowds for his sermons?

Those who most wished to promote him engaged in denial. After his early death it was claimed that he hadn't really died at all. The stories range from the official versions of resurrection in the New Testament to apocryphal accounts of his being spirited away at the last minute to India, but the effect is the same: *Jesus couldn't have been a loser because losing is bad.* Even after hearing him say things like: "To gain your life you must lose it."

Losing *is* bad. We feel this in our bones. It is the equivalent of the Evil Eye—we ward it off with jogging, diet, extra courses. We practise positive thinking—puffing "I think I can," like the Little Choo Choo, keeping positive thoughts in our heads, doing affirmations and even keeping little bits of magic about us—crystals, holy water, and so on. But you know what? All that stuff doesn't really work, because in our deepest hearts we know that losing is inevitable. We can run as fast as we wish, empty the health food store of vitamins, psychically numb ourselves until we are more like machines than people, but the loss we are avoiding is as near as our own shadow. We can feel its clammy breath on our necks even at the height of our success.

Have you ever known a really good loser? I've known several, and their influence on my life is—I would have to say—greater than the influence of the winners. There is a certain quality of serenity around those whose paths have taken them through a great fall from which they have lived to tell the tale.

One such beautiful loser was a colleague, a fellow minister. I am very anxious to conceal his identity, not because I think he would mind you knowing who he was, but because he was always a modest man. I will call him Mike.

Mike was from a London working class family. He was born during the Blitz and was too young to send away to Somerset for safety. He grew up during the optimistic days after the war, and began to have ambitions beyond working in a factory. He studied and became a minister in the Congregationalist church, and did very well. He was a Christian, but he was also a career man; I think *being a minister* was more important to him than *ministering*, if you know what I mean.

He married a little late in life, finally yielding to the expectations of society about a clergyman needing a family. He had two children. He had a church and a life and everything was okay. Except for one thing:

Mike was gay. He said later that he thought anyone could have told him this except his closest friends and family, but he didn't even know it himself. He was living in a thick cocoon of denial. It just wasn't on for a Congregationalist minister to be homosexual, and so he had to lie. Not just to his church, his wife and family: to *himself.*

This lie made Mike keep secrets. These secrets hurt the people who loved him by depriving them of the truth. And these secrets—banished into the cellar of his life, began to take on a life of their own. The urge to express himself as a gay man led him one day to a public men's room, where he was entrapped by a policeman and charged with public indecency. He was ruined, in the sense that we use the term. He was dismissed from his church, evicted from the roll of ministers and unemployed. His marriage quickly collapsed, and so did his self-esteem. As a result of self-hatred, he wasn't careful, and he contracted the HIV virus. For years he lived a marginal life, consumed by shame and blame. He worked at low-paying jobs as long as he could and lived on the dole. In the familiar words, Mike went all the way down.

He later said that when he reached rock bottom, there was nothing left but his religion, and his identification with Jesus grew. He found that he was growing a sense of vocation that he hadn't had when he was a "winner." One day he went into a Unitarian chapel in east London, and he stayed. Later, he began to take services, and finally—three years later, he became a Unitarian minister.

When I met Mike, he had advanced into full-blown AIDS. He was pale and thin and used a walking stick. He had a dense Cockney accent and sometimes annoyed me with his too-Christian language. My first impression was that the denomination had made a mistake: this guy was too orthodox in his beliefs, he was no intellectual, and was clearly too ill to be effective.

But Mike was very easy to be around. He had a certain quality I've known before in beautiful losers. He was not self-abasing or mock modest; he could give you a pretty good argument if he disagreed with you. But he was genuine and calm, and when he spoke, you knew he was giving you the whole truth as he understood it—not editing it for your consumption, not putting any extra spin on it at all. Just the unvarnished truth. It made him a superb pastoral minister, as I've heard many people say. As a preacher, he was able to communicate with everybody, even though his voice was unlovely and his ideas a bit outmoded. People loved him; he loved them back. He was in his own church for just ten months, during which time the numbers tripled. When he died, his funeral was packed.

Mike was one of those people who have come through the fire. He was a loser in nearly every method of keeping score. He never recovered his family, his lost friends, his income. He never had a miracle recovery from AIDS. Hardly anybody will remember him for long. But I knew something about him as soon as I saw him, and he helped me learn something I'd maybe rather have been ignorant of for the rest of my life: *it is in losing that we really grow.*

The Indian spiritual master Meher Baba described a condition known to Hindus as *satyanashi*. He was especially fond of people who have suffered "sudden inexplicable ruin" like my friend Mike. *Satyanashi* means in Sanskrit, "destruction of power." About this, Baba said, "It is not spirituality, but a precursor to the spiritual path." "The ravaging of the garden of your life" he said, leads a soul toward real spiritual growth. When I once talked about it to some Hindu friends, they reacted in shock. If they had been Catholics they would have crossed themselves. "Don't even talk about it," they'd say. As if ruin, the big time of losing, was contagious. The Evil Eye.

I've been lucky enough to have known some beautiful losers in my life. And I've had the opportunity of losing out a few times myself. Not enough to represent "ravaging of the garden of my heart," but enough so that for a while my life became an open book and any chance of subterfuge vanished. It is a strange experience. If you've never had it, let me recommend it to you. When you find yourself in a situation where no amount of excuses or spin doctoring can get you off the hook, you find that the pain of embarrassment is more than made up for by the sheer pleasure of being known.

That's worth repeating: *being known.* Many think—and I am one of them—that this *being known* is the nearest desire to the human heart. Perhaps that's why we substitute the craving for fame and reputation for the real thing. And if we think we can only be known through great achievements or beauty or position in society, perhaps that's why we so hate to fail.

What are we afraid of, really? Being discovered to be weak, vulnerable, corruptible, insecure? Of being found out? Well, that's just three letters away from the heartfelt desire of us all: being *found.* Being found to be human. Being ourselves, being known.

Don't take this to mean that we need to get stuck into dangerous balancing acts and feats of dare-devilry to enhance our chances of failing. We are doing enough of that already. What I would recommend is that we make it a little easier for people not to succeed, not to win all the time, especially the children. There are better ways of becoming known than having to fall from a very great height. We need to start at the bottom, in our relationships inside and out of the family. The way we do that is to show others a little bit of our own weakness and inadequacy. It empowers them, and that's a good thing.

And—as we all somehow discover—it feels like the truth. It hurts good.

Me and My Shadow

I've got a friend called Terencio. He is that rarest of things—an African Spaniard. He came to Britain all alone, not able to speak English, and he still can't, despite trying to study every day. The unfamiliar sounds just seem to escape him. Nevertheless, he manages to find odd jobs, and after a long wait, has got himself a flat in South London.

Terencio is a member of a fringe fundamentalist church that has a Spanish service on Saturdays—the Sabbath, according to them. Terencio spends about five hours there in prayer and singing, and he carries his Bible everywhere he goes. He is very worried about my soul. You see, Terencio believes that the Devil is lurking everywhere to haul people down to Hell. He once told me that the average pub contained two or three demons and a disco five or six. They are there to lure people through their base desires into an acceptance of the Evil One, and start them on the long slippery slope. He thinks that modern people like me might be particularly vulnerable to this process, and—given our traditional scorn for such superstitions—he might just have a point.

People like Terencio believe that what we think of as the dark side of life must be avoided at all costs. Salvation lies in denying the Devil access to one's soul, suppressing negative feelings, avoiding thoughts that are impure, keeping the company of the saved. His theology is rather like a Zoroastrian one, featuring two great cosmic forces—God and Satan, pitted in a great battle for the world, with the outcome still unclear. Christianity had its own version of this, through what was called the Pelagian heresy. This leads to the notion that, by always walking on the sunny side of the street—avoiding the shade—one might escape the clutches of evil and ally oneself with God.

Before dismissing this idea as absurd, we probably need to see how much it resembles our own attitudes. Present day depth psychologists tell us that we too have evolved ways of staying on the sunny side of the street, avoiding the Devil. Only we don't call it the Devil anymore. It has a new name, and increasingly we are staring to recognise it—it's called the *shadow*.

When I was a child there was a wonderful radio drama that came on late Sunday afternoon. A man named Lamont Cranston could make himself invisible and penetrate the dark deeds of criminals. When he came on the air, he always said, "Who knows what evil lurks in the hearts of men? (mad laughter) Only the Shadow knows!" It was thrilling, and now—I think—prophetic.

About the same time, C.G. Jung was putting the finishing touches on his own concept of the shadow. Breaking away from the Freudian view that the darkness in humanity emanates from that cesspool of the unconscious called the *Id*, Jung said that the shadow is something that all people have. It's part of basic human equipment, like hair and teeth. The shadow is rather like a room in our unconscious minds, where we shove everything we don't want to know about ourselves. From the earliest days of infancy we are growing not just in visible personality, but in shadow as well. When we learn, as we do, that "good boys don't steal," then we—in order to be good boys—hide the impulse to nick sweets out of our sight, in the shadow. If we are told that "nice girls don't have sexual impulses," the same thing happens. Our venality and our lusts, not appropriate for the mask or persona that we learn to wear for the world, pile up in a kind of glory hole of the psyche, and little by little develop into an alternate source of personality. I don't mean anything like "The Three Faces of Eve" and other such psychological horror stories. Jung was quick to point out that these unconscious accumulations of material weren't real, separate selves, but something like *themes* that produced moods and desires outside the conscious reach of the normal personality.

In cases like those of my friend Terencio, there is a phenomenon known as "backsliding." This is when someone, exhausted by the process of denial, lets everything rip at once and charges gleefully into the pubs and discos to meet the demons. The limiting of the personality to just the good and acceptable—avoiding sin, as it were—tires you out. We might notice this in ourselves, when, weary and lacking focus, we might lash out at someone or gorge on chocolates or utter a racist epithet, something we might not normally do. Sometimes the Shadow is content with time-sharing. A well-known theologian, creator of some of the best-loved Christian thinking of the last century, was revealed after his death by his own wife to have been a fairly busy shadow owner. Among his rich stash of pornography were found trophies of his secret sexual conquests. Avoiding the Devil is the narrowest of tightropes, and everybody slips.

In other theologies, the fallen angel Satan is not as powerful as God. He got into trouble when—as the best loved of the lieutenants—he got over-ambitious and fell from grace. He has been on a several million-year sulk, and the end times will be a moment of reconciliation with God, who longs for his return. This is no doubt due to the fact that when Satan went AWOL, he took some of the very best things about creation along with him.

In the microcosmic universe of the self, we can understand this. When we are nothing but pure and dutiful citizens, relying only on "wholesome" entertainment like that which the Disney Empire peddles, when we never express undainty or "immoral" attributes, when we have polished our harps until they glow in the dark, life begins to lose its flavour. My father once remarked on the fact that our pet dog preferred drinking out of mud puddles to quenching his thirst in the sanitary dog bowl. He said, "Dirty water tastes better." I know what he meant. Don't you?

But it is not just the flavour of life that is lost through the depositing of bits of ourselves in the cellar of the shadow. Whole new ways of healing have evolved through what is called "shadow work." It seems that when we put away attributes and impulses that we don't want to accept about ourselves, we are also losing access to bits that make for the best in us as well, and some practitioners are addressing this directly. They take as their inspiration the wisdom of the Sufi story in which Mullah Nasruddin is seen searching in his front garden for a lost key. A neighbour stops to help. After ten fruitless minutes, the neighbour asks, "Where did you drop the key, exactly?"

"In the house," says Nasruddin.

"Then why are we looking for it out here?" asks the frustrated neighbour.

"There's more light out here," answers Nasruddin.

Looking in only the bright bits of our lives can't answer all our questions; we have to go into where there's the least light to find what we need.

Shadow work can be a liberating experience, if not one for the fainthearted. It is not that we necessarily need therapy, although I have often benefited from it. I might say, "Don't knock it until you've tried it." It isn't really a matter of being "sick" or "disturbed" or any of those things. It has much more to do with the urge to wholeness. What we are talking about here may have the name of psychology, but it is really more to do with soul, and the spiritual search.

Much has been said about "integrating" the shadow into the personality, and that sounds about right. The real hero isn't interested in conquering mountains, but in ascending awareness; not scuba-diving, but pearl fishing in the mysterious pool of the heart; not slaying dragons, but killing the lies we have so long told ourselves. And not merely accepting the flaws and dark urges that we all know we have, but in actively identifying with them.

And how does one go about that? Surely not, as in the case of Terencio and his companions, by tilting, charging into the bars to meet the demons. Nor in the pursuit of psychic espionage through a secret life. These are more a matter of inattention to one's real needs than any sort of brave approach to mystery.

I think it is more a matter of self-observation, and—paradoxically—that happens best in company. Let's face it: our shadow sides are much better known to those around us than to ourselves. Our petty fears and awkwardness, our small acts of cruelty, our defensiveness, denial and lying, our addictions and phobias are more obvious to our companions than we like to think. The theologian's wife will have had an inkling. Unlike our birth families, our communities are chosen by us. To the extent that we enter them willingly and gain confidence in our acceptance we are enabling the process of self-revelation, and in the kind chemistry of community are made gently aware of where we have still to go. It is not an easy business, but how else could it be?

The last chapter of the Bible that will be written some day, I think, has to do with the romance of God and his pal Satan burying the hatchet and falling into each other's arms. The bright side and the dark side reconciled. The human personality made whole in the final gift of growth and struggle. Every time we shine a little light into our own dark cellars, or enable someone else to do so by active love and trust, we are uttering a fragment of that tale. No, it's not easy, but, as they say, it's the only game in town. Have we really got anything better to do?

Tall Mast, Deep Keel

Have you ever seen a sailboat out of the water? If you haven't, it might surprise you. Go down to a marina sometime and have a look at all those boats rocking in their slips, their high aluminium masts, and the clinking of the sheets and lines against the metal. When the sails are hoisted, you see a marvel of light, airy substance thrown up into the sunlight, trembling with every breeze. The sailboat seems composed of air, as every square centimetre reaches for the invisible wind.

But take this same boat out of the water, haul it up with a crane into dry dock and the illusion of lightness disappears. Beneath the water line, reaching not up for the wind, but down for the muddy depths, you'll see the keel. The hull is not bright and white like the upper boat. It is rank with clinging seaweed and barnacle. The keel in a large boat will have tons of lead inside, pulling the craft toward the sea bed. It will look heavy. And it will be surprisingly deep, because if you want to have a tall mast, you've got to have a deep keel. That's just a rule of boat building. If you want all that lovely, airy stuff topside, you've got to have dark, heavy stuff below the surface. If you don't, you'll capsize.

Ever since people started travelling about using the wind as an engine, the metaphor of human striving will have been present. The invisible force that can ruffle your hair or flatten your house is the model most often used to describe the Spirit. In Greek, the wind is *pneuma*, the word also used for *spirit*. In Hebrew, it is *ruah*, which also means both *wind* and *spirit*. The light, invisible, unpredictable force leaps the confines of the physical world into the metaphysical. The wind, as Jesus famously said, "listeth where it will, and no one can say whence it sprang and whither it bloweth." Like the spirit of God, the Holy Spirit. You can build windmills to mill your grain and erect high sails to propel you over the water, but you cannot predict, and much less, control it. The Spirit also comes and goes, touching things with meaning for a moment, and then leaving them again.

You might extend this metaphor just a wee bit and say that religious practice is a kind of sail we erect to catch this spirit. The cloth we stitch, the ropes we tie, the masts we send up are prayers and poetry and song. And sometimes we catch it; it luffs in our jibs and billows in our mainsails and we are sent without apparent effort across the sea of uncertainty in which we live. But sometimes we are, as sailors say, "in irons", locked in the doldrums of confusion and doubt, and the spirit doesn't come. In these moments all the cleverness of sail building just doesn't help; the wind is still, and we come to an apparent halt with it. And sometimes, too, the wind comes in an unexpected way. It blows with great force and there is something like terror there, something to send you to your knees, something to make you shed canvas, something to remind you of the awe and power that is also present in this wind, this spirit.

Our top parts are always reaching for this wind. What we call our spirit, the striving for the universal and the absolute is a tall mast. It is also the most visible part of us, the part we most choose to reveal. If you're out sailing far from shore, "blue water" sailing, as they say, the first thing you will see of another sailboat is its sail, appearing over the curvature of the earth. And almost certainly, the first thing you will know of another person is what she does: architect, doctor, housewife. What interesting achievements he has to his credit: clubs, degrees, honours. And in this we see the way the person reaches for the sky, what ambitions drive his boat.

In religious practice this reaching is also toward the sky, trying to hoist ourselves out of the mundane in the direction of the infinite, to some great point of resolution, some oneness, some heaven. We set our sails, we tack and jibe, run and reach, seeking the last great port of call. But as our sails reach up, our keels reach downward, heavily dragging us back from where we sprang. Holding us in the feared depths, the lair of monsters and the unknown, Davy Jones' locker. This is the deep water, the home, not of spirit, but of *soul*.

It appears that this word is a mystery to us. When we speak of soul, we may imagine some little white thing that is somehow connected with us. In Spain, when people sneeze, others say "Jesus!" in case the soul is blown out of the body by the breath. In Hindu cremations, the skull is broken by a stick to allow the soul to fly. In Russia, even in the cold, a window is always left open as an exit in the house of a person who has died.

Christian theology has been very remiss in matters of the soul, which is why we often use the terms *spirit* and *soul* interchangeably. The soul in theology is the part of us that exists before our birth and survives our death, we are told. Or, as the Hindus would have it, *atma* is always part of *paramatma*, the *oversoul*. For most of us, when we think of it at all, the soul is something vague that may or may not exist, that has more to do with African American music or cuisine than the core part of ourselves.

The writer Thomas Moore—the modern fellow, not the "man for all seasons"—writes in his book *The Care of the Soul*[1] about an interesting moment in Christian history. This is the moment of the baptism of the Rabbi Jesus by the wild prophet John the Baptist. This takes place, we are told, in the River Jordan. We see two men standing waist deep in the water. Above, in the bright air, resides the spirit, betokened by the appearance of a dove. But below lies the muddy water of this river, pointing, says Moore, to the other half of the human story, the soul.

To some extent it seems that poor old Jesus has been kidnapped and held hostage for centuries by those advocates of half a theology we call the church. The focus is upon transcendence, spiritualisation of life, escape from a broken world of sorrows into an abstract infinite, leaving behind the rough and tumble, the injustice and impermanence of human life. Jesus was made an unwilling conspirator in this game of

---

1. Thomas Moore, *The Care of the Soul: A Guide for Cultivating Depth and Sacredness In Everyday Life,* Harper Collins, New York, NY, 1992

spiritualisation and escape. His words were reported to point upward toward the sky, and leave behind the life below the water line. Perhaps we should go looking there, holding our breath, conquering our fear of the dark and diving deep into soul and soulfulness.

When we go looking for soul, we need to start where there is certain quality of being. This is the realm of poetry, of dreams and reflection, and—yes—of sensual awareness. We need to start where sunset is not just refracted dust motes in the atmosphere, and where laughter is not just a predictable reaction of neurological spasm. We need to look for what flamenco musicians call *duende*. We need to see what lives in every one of the mundane events, muddy, salty, rough and sweet events, the texture of our lives. Not to focus on the sails and mast, but on the barnacles and brine beneath us.

In our search for soulfulness, we may find benefits we haven't yet imagined, but also risks we haven't yet dared. The writer James Hillman speaks of "psychic numbing" as the result of abandoning the approach to soulfulness. The world doesn't need any more spiritualisation, he says; it has far too much already. Spirit has a dark face as well as a bright countenance. The longing for spirit leads us in an increasingly abstract direction. The attempt to dissolve the particular in the universal is where things like intercontinental ballistic missiles have their birth. Population planning, medical rationing, civil defence strategies all contain elements of this "numbing" of the soul. We may reduce humans to ciphers, tragedies to "acceptable loss ratios" if we abstract and spiritualise our thinking too far. And that is where religion most often fails us; it sends us too far from where our souls attain compassion.

I remember once, while working in Botswana, reading about a conference concerning the distribution of emergency foodstuffs in an emergency caused by drought. People like me, with degrees and Land Rovers, discussed patterns of nutritional risk areas, and heard how the people in charge made decisions. It all seemed very fair and rational to me at the time. About that same time I was working with a few remote medical clinics, mostly as an "odd bod" that did some driving. I noticed that most of the babies who turned up at the clinic were looking pretty sickly, even though we were not in a high-risk area as defined by the experts. My friend Mma Mosala explained it very simply: "There is no milk."

I thought about this, and being as psychically numbed as anybody, tried to see the skinny little bodies of the children as part of a controlled system of distribution and risk analysis. It didn't work. Even if I didn't look at the babies, I could hear them. My wife started carrying cartons of UHT milk along, and would just hand them out. I argued that this was a senseless act of no lasting consequence, and she'd just give me a certain look. It was the way the soul looks at you when you are sailing around in the abstract. So one day we got in the Mazda pickup truck and drove into town, where I had a strange interview with a lower grade minister of government. He patiently explained to me about rationing, planning and so on, but I just sat there smiling. He was ignoring my wife, and every time I looked at her she just shook her head. At last the minister sighed a great sigh and said "How much do you want?" Before I could answer, Barbara said, "How much have you got?"

Two hours later we had loaded the Mazda to the spring rupturing point in a warehouse where men wore masks so they wouldn't breathe too much powdered milk dust. We took the milk to Mogoditshane Red Cross and just left it there. Mma Mosala was probably grateful, but if she was, she was too kind to show it. I knew, Barbara knew and she knew that the milk had gone where it was meant to. The soul made a decision that the spirit couldn't fathom.

The soul's home is the sacred part of ourselves. The soul is no literalist, requiring set answers. It seeks the depth of experience, the slow and thorough discovery of truth, peeling away the onion layers of mere facts to reveal not explanations, but meaning. Like the child asking again to be told the same old story, the soul does not feed on novelty—much less on factual formulae, but on the shape and texture of things. At its darkest reaches it tends to irrationality—this is one of its risks—but it is here that we need the countervailing influence of spirit. The dread of the irrational, the fear of slipping into some state of near bestiality is what prevents many of our much-needed forays into soul work.

It is a poor thing to live without spirituality, without the reach for the infinite. But I believe it is a worse thing to live without soul. I say that because what I see around me is loss of soul on all sides as we float into cyberspace, rig tall masts and ignore our keels, try to live without seeing and without feeling. When we do that, meaning becomes just another word, confused with explanation. And wisdom disappears under a fluttering tide of mere information.

I long for the return of those days I have had and lost, when the meaning of things was revealed by their very essence, when the clang of a church bell or the feel of dew on the railings communicated to me more than all the explanations in the world. I do not know when I had these things, nor indeed, when I lost them. Maybe it's a memory of something, not lost at all, but yet to come. And maybe this longing is an important clue to my own search for meaning and wholeness. Maybe what seems to be an ordinary life is really more than that. Maybe it is a laboratory of the soul, and by taking a few risks, we may slip together over the side, leaving the mast for the keel, and find ourselves again.

Getting Out of the Wu Wei

Here's a true story a friend of mine told me recently. I can't remember all the details exactly; but then, that's why a story is a story and not a scientific document. A noted guest speaker on Eastern religion was giving a workshop at a London church. The afternoon had gone well, full of insights and good will. A few people had stayed on after the seminar and spoken at some length with the guest. They decided to adjourn to a nearby coffee shop to continue talking.

When they left the church building, two Buddhist monks were standing on the pavement with begging bowls. Each bowl had a few coins inside. The speaker approached one of them. He reached into the bowl and took out a twenty-pence piece, said, "Thank you," and put it into his shirt pocket. The monk nodded. The others were stunned, but said nothing. They followed the speaker into the coffee shop and, after a few minutes forgot about the incident and once again became engaged in conversation about Zen, the Tao, and other topics.

When the coffee shop closed a few hours later, the group came out onto the street into a rainstorm. Some of the participants lived a good distance away, and they decided to catch a taxi. No one had a mobile phone, but there was a phone box a few yards away. The problem was, no one had any change, having given it all to their long-suffering waiter. By now, the till was closed in the coffee shop. They faced a good soaking. The guest speaker said nothing, but, smiling, reached into his top pocket and offered the coin he had taken from the monk's bowl.

I have no trouble believing that this really happened, even though the details are now clouded. I have no trouble believing it because I have experienced similar incidents in my own life. You know what I mean: those little co-incidences that happen that make sense in the moment and then are quickly forgotten. A seemingly meaningless event, such as missing a train, causes you to meet the love of your life. A low score in a certain exam due to a head cold changes your life's work, for better or worse. A classified advert glimpsed in a newspaper left on a bus leads to the purchase of a beloved home. Our lives are full of these things, whether we notice them or not. I am willing to bet that any of us could come up with a half-dozen examples right now if we really thought about it.

The speaker in the story could have anticipated neither the rainstorm nor the lack of pocket change. He almost certainly had no idea what taking the monk's coin might lead to. He was acting in a way that defies ideas of normal behaviour. You might even say that he was acting *mindlessly*.

People who have studied or practised Eastern religions, such as Taoism or Zen Buddhism, will know that "mindlessness"—something to be avoided in Western culture—is a key element in the path to enlightenment. In Chinese, it could be translated as *wu wei*, literally meaning, "no mind." *Wu wei* does not mean madness, as when someone "loses their mind." Madness is probably a condition of too much mind, not too little. And it doesn't mean mere ignorance, either.

Lao Tze was the founder of Taoism. His classic series of poems, or reflections, the *Tao Te Ching*, forms the heart of the religion or philosophy (there is debate over which word is more appropriate). Lao Tze was what he was known as, but it was not his real name. The words translate as "Old Boy." This is an appropriate oxymoron, because his writings about the ultimate reality, or *Tao*, are a series of paradoxes. Weakness is strength, for example: the supple and yielding willow is better able to survive winds than the mighty oak. Humility is power: the sea is the "king of all waters" because it lies below the others. Mindlessness, or *wu wei*, is knowledge, because the *Tao*, or life force, is unknowable. Shot through the teachings of Taoism is the idea that all things are part of Tao, yet Tao is more than the sum of all things. Wisdom lies in leaving behind the notion that the limited mind is in control, and beginning to accommodate the flow of Tao. In other words, getting out of the way.

Lao Tze was influenced by Buddhism, and so to students of that religion it may be necessary to point out that "mindlessness" is not contrary to the Buddhist injunction of "mindfulness" in all behaviour. Mindfulness means being observant, applying attention to what happens without the idea that one is controlling it. The apparent contradiction is more of a statement about the inadequacy of the English language than an indictment of Eastern thought. To Westerners—maybe especially to Unitarians—"mind" is a wholly wonderful thing. Unitarianism is often described as the religion where you do not have to leave your mind at the door. We associate the mind with the gift of rational thought and inventiveness, and in that we are correct. What we don't often address in the West is the other face of the mind—the seat of the limited ego, the "little self" that makes exclusivist claims on reality and on all other life forms.

The ego is the centre of the world, as far as *it* is concerned. Meher Baba once pointed out the three main statements of the limited self as: "I am unique," "I am preferred," and "I have a right to live." This represents a disconnected self, bouncing around in a universe of foreign objects, competing for resources, struggling for control, and trying to evade death. Satisfaction results from a series of temporary, small victories: wealth, power, and the attention of others, all of which the larger self knows are fleeting and ultimately insignificant.

But we are not just our egos, despite its insistent clamouring for supremacy. There is love, that entirely irrational force that seems to soften the hard edges of our personalities. There is hope, whose whole existence is based on proclaiming the logically improbable possible. But there is also something else. Call it a hunch or an intuition. Call it *chi* or *prana* or the Holy Spirit—it has lots of names. Lao Tze called it the Tao. The *Tao Te Ching, or* the *Way of Life,* is about this thing, whatever it is.

Let's put some modern words into the "Old Boy's" mouth. Let's put it something like this: before we were, while we are, after we have ceased to be is this something. We can't name it, so we'll call it the Tao. It is not merely bigger than we are; it *is* who we really are. The Tao has its own way of working, a way that is not just unknown to us, but which is unknowable. It blows like a fresh wind through every tiny event, every formation of suns and planets, and can be heard in every bird's song and urban squeal of brakes. It is beyond any conception we may have of good or evil; its existence is sufficient. It cannot be blocked, nor can it be enhanced by our actions. It is not foreign to our souls, because it is our soul. What happens does so because it must; it always would have happened, whatever we may have thought about it. Wisdom lies in the identification with Tao, not with our small concerns. Real happiness lies in giving permission—no, more—in giving *blessing* to the inevitable. That is the way of life.

I don't know if you're like me, but that idea fills me with mixed emotions. On the one hand, I can feel the hissing of my ego—the one supreme and important Arthur G. Lester—denying and simultaneously fearing the concept. On the other—can you feel it, too?—there is a delicious intuition forming, a kind of irrational joy. I get the same feeling when I hear Jesus say, "Take no heed of the morrow" and "Don't concern yourself with what you will have to eat; the Father knows when even a sparrow falls," or when the great Rumi says, "Give up to grace. The Ocean takes care of each wave till it gets to shore." Then the mind comes along again, that old party pooper, saying, as Sigmund Freud did, "That's just leftover infantile fantasy." Or poor Karl Marx, shivering in the British Library, assuring me that this is just an opiate for me and the masses. They won't shut up, but recently their cawing cynicism has become fainter. I can hear the laughter of the merry "Old Boy" much more distinctly.

It comes back again and again to that elusive word "faith," doesn't it? Faith is defined in the Bible as "the substance of things hoped for, the evidence of things unseen." You either have it or you don't. It can comfort you in times of affliction and make you optimistic when things are all right. It doesn't matter much to the Tao, though. It just goes on wending its way through eternity, like the wind "listing where it will." Your wave will be carried to shore in its own time, with or without your consent.

But maybe you're like me. Maybe that idea of giving blessing to the Tao, or spirit, has really begun to grab you. Maybe you have a hunch that the way things work out is a cause for celebration, even worship. Maybe you want to do more than grudgingly assent; you want to sing about it, too. Maybe you want to make this fledgling faith, or hunch, work its way into your daily life.

Faith is meaningless if it doesn't enliven the way you spend your days. It might get you through the "night sweats," but it will not do what it's intended for, really—to unite the eternal and the temporary. If you believe that something is working itself out through the universe, then it is working its way out in your life, too. If there is a bigger "plan" or whatever, aiding it is not just sensible, but joyous. There's a definition of practical faith for you.

So we come back to the place where Lao Tze started from. We need advice on how to work with this force, which blows through us. Maybe we need rules to help us out. Here are a few tips from the "Old Boy."

1. *Don't be crafty*. It may seem that we need to scheme and manipulate in order to get what we want. In a limited way, that's true. If you grind money out of others, you'll have more than they do. The problem is, you probably won't know how to use it; your satisfaction will come from scheming and winning, and that—as they used to say about chewing gum—loses its flavour on the bedpost overnight.

Yes, Mohammed was right: trust in God and tie up your camel at night. You don't want to be a liability by wandering around aimlessly in traffic. Be sensible, but keep in mind the goal of participating in the saga of creation, not just in your own fleeting little story.

2. *Be observant*. The little miracles, such as the appearance of the Buddhist's coin, happen all the time. But these are merely co-inci-

dences in the random universe of your ego's private nightmare. Patterns are patterns because they are forms that recur. Go out of your house expecting to be led by the Tao and you will be.

3. *Don't be choosy.* Not only things you like will come along. There will be road accidents, heart attacks, tooth decay. The Tao isn't like a genie in the bottle. As the tee-shirt reminds us, "Shit happens." Reacting with fear and resentment not only doesn't help, it actually prevents the growth we are all seeking. And besides, how many times has something apparently awful turned out to be a good thing in the long run? I'm not singing the old song about silver linings; I'm saying, try to see whatever occurs as part of a story that hasn't been told yet.

4. *Look in strange places.* Archimedes had troubles we can't imagine. The king tortured him and threatened to harm his family unless he came up with a way to assess the value of gold. His wife told him, "Look, Archie, why don't you have a nice hot bath." He did, and after taking his mind off the problem—Eureka!—he came up with the theory of displacement.

5. *Relax.* That's just the best advice possible, isn't it?

We free thinkers are very tolerant. We learn from all the great world religions, from Marcus Aurelius and Maimonides to L. Ron Hubbard and even Bob Dylan. But we've got a blind spot. We don't pay much attention to evangelical Christianity of the "happy-clappy" kind. But the other day, as I was trying to work my way through this chapter, I saw a phrase of theirs that could have saved a lot of argument. It's the phrase, "Let go and let God." I guess I've worked my way around to that at last. I couldn't say it much better than that.

Eros the Healer

The Greek god Eros, known to the Romans as Cupid, was the son of Aphrodite, the goddess of love. Some people, however, think he was not her son, but her assistant, having himself been born from Chaos in the very beginning of the world. This means that he is either a very old, and therefore a very important god, or a younger, less important one. In the same way, Aphrodite has two possible origins: she is either "Ourania," which means "heavenly" or "Pandemos," which means, "vulgar, of the people." Eros is therefore seen as one of two distinct persons, depending upon the observer. In one aspect, he is a sly troublemaker, going around at night shooting arrows that break up families and wreak havoc with society. It is this Eros that we are most familiar with: a beguiling but dangerous imp who needs to be locked out of the sanctity of hearth and home. He is a kind of wicked joke. That silly little statue in Piccadilly Circus speaks of the comical esteem in which he is generally held.

But Eros has another, largely forgotten, face. In one of the seminal myths of Western civilisation, he was sent by Aphrodite to make the beautiful Psyche (the root of the word for soul) fall in love with a certain mortal. Psyche, however, falls in love with Eros, who has an affair with her. He makes her agree that she will never look at his face, because he is immortal and she is human, but one night she lights a lamp and sees him, with grave consequences. The affair ends with Aphrodite in a rage. She makes Psyche perform a series of apparently impossible errands to avoid death. Psyche manages to complete all these tasks and ultimately becomes a god herself. This myth has become a central archetype in what is often called "sacred psychology," in which myths become maps of the human soul.

Eros' dual nature has always confounded humanity. On the one hand, he is a minor criminal, whose role, if any, is to make couples fall in love. Once that is accomplished, he is banished, kept locked out of the house. On the other, he is the active principle of love, the force that makes the soul go on to perform the Herculean tasks assigned to it—the return through the maze of experience to its divine origin. The first, minor Eros, who is legislated against and deemed improper by a controlling society, is the one who represents mere lust and infatuation. When I was researching this chapter on the Internet, every other listing for Eros, or erotic, was for a pornographic web site. That's how closely associated he has become with vice and naughtiness. The other Eros has been largely ignored and forgotten, and it is this one that I want to find here. That one I call Eros the Healer.

Eros the Healer is one of life's most enduring gods, representing not only sexual passion but our own sensual connectedness with the earth and everything that lives on it. If love is at the root of all major religions, then Eros, its active principle, cannot be excluded from them. To exclude Eros from one's life is to lose touch with the physical and emotional world, to lock out and alienate the soul.

Erotic sensibility is with us at birth and stays with us until our last breath. However it is denied, legislated against, or frowned upon, it is never wholly controllable. The church leapt on the prudery of St. Augustine, that same chap who gave us the absurdity of "original sin," because they needed to gain dominance over Dionysian and other renegade cults that were competing with Christianity during the reign of Constantine. The erotic impulse was simply too liberating; it challenged the hegemony of church law. It had to be relegated to the dustbin, and so became synonymous with sin. What Adam and Eve were doing all day in the Garden was perfectly all right with God. Their state of undress was not a problem. What was a problem was the beginning of self-consciousness, symbolised by the eating of the fruit of the tree of the knowledge of good and evil. Ignoring this, the church set about making sexuality a ticket to Hell; thus began a long term of exile for the whole human race, not just from a lost archetypal garden, but from ourselves.

Matthew Fox, in his groundbreaking book, *Original Blessing*,[2] speaks about "erotic justice." I mentioned this at a meeting of church elders once and got a dressing down from one of the attendees. He was bristling with outraged virtue; it seems I had inadvertently exceeded his tolerance threshold. I tried to explain that Fox wasn't talking about sex, but about a way of promoting justice through compassion and empathy with the accused and the victims alike. He wasn't impressed—he just insisted that I would never make any headway with churchgoers if I used "unsuitable language" like that. Maybe he was right; the jury's still out on that one.

One of the most common images of Western civilisation has always been the figure of Justice, represented as a woman, usually carrying a sword with which to split legal hairs, and very often wearing a blindfold. This odd feature is a testimony to the Hellenic notion that true justice should be blind, meaning unswayed by appearances and extraneous influences.

Contrast this with the ancient Hebrew courts, in which the judge was supposed not only to be able to see but to have the sharpness of vision to really look into a situation. Think of old Solomon, peering out of damp eyes at the predicament of the two claimants to the baby, and his compassionate solution. A judge that cannot see into the hearts of litigants, one who is incapable of erotic justice, is no judge at all. People are not ciphers to be examined clinically. They are like all of humanity: sweaty, confused, proud, ashamed, capable of change or damned. They need to be understood, and understanding comes only from seeing what they see and feeling what they feel. The purpose of justice is to make right what is wrong. Wanting blind justice is like hiring a blind coach driver; it may be politically correct to hire disabled people, but you'd have to be crazy to do it in this case. It is similar to appointing a bunch of male private school graduates, who've never

---

2. Matthew Fox, *Original Blessing*, Bear and Company, Santa Fe, N.M.,1983

been short of a square meal in their lives, to sit in judgement on working-class ghetto kids. You know, powdered wigs and all. But that's probably another chapter.

Michel Foucault writes about the earliest sex crimes in modern European history. These were all but non-existent until the latter part of the eighteenth century. It is interesting that this was also the era of the first censuses. With the advance of machine production, governments began to make the workforce—that is, the population—its business. And near the heart of population control was the control of sexuality. Control sexuality and you control humanity—almost. But the stirrings of Eros will out, even if the appearance is perverse and unhealthy. This is where lap dancing, heavy telephone breathers, and Thai sex junkets have their beginnings.

When I speak of reclaiming the erotic, I'm not speaking of mere sex. (Is sex mere?) I'm speaking about the entire sensual self, the love of embracing nature. Of Willie Nelson's deathless lines about cowboys who "love cool mountain mornings and warm puppies," as well as "girls of the night." Of Oriah Mountain Dreamer's "smell of the sea and salt of our tears." We have an erotic experience when we slip into a welcome hot bath in a steamy bathroom scented with some frivolous aroma from the supermarket, when we zip our parkas and head up a rocky path in the fog, when we tear into fresh-baked bread from the oven. We do not have an erotic experience when we gulp a bitter packaged sandwich on the pavement, anaesthetise ourselves with spirits, or stick our faces into paperbacks on the train to avoid the odium and tedium of urban life.

When I get to my cabin in Spain, it always takes me two days to arrive. I may be there technically, but I am still really somewhere else in my head. I always seem to carry batteries so that I can tune into the BBC World Service in case I get bored or lonely. I spend the first night reading some detective novel and stay up late, listening for strange rustlings outside. I am confronting the environment, not dancing with it.

The descent into myself is gradual. By the second day, I notice that I am not merely dosing myself in the morning with caffeine, but actually savouring my coffee. Cooking becomes not a problem, but a pleasure. Peeling onions in the mountain twilight is fun. After a while I begin to enjoy the strain on my thigh muscles as I walk up the trail, and set my pace accordingly. The day becomes full, even though there are apparently fewer things in it than a workday at the office. I am having an erotic experience, a sensual love affair with the physical world. It is not all pleasure—neither is love—but it is real. It focuses me, calms me, makes me compose lines of bad poetry in my head. This is one of the acknowledged gifts of Eros: he makes everybody a poet.

The local people, just emerging from a poor peasant life, have kept some of this alive in their culture. I remember being unnerved years ago to see how men interacted with children, their own and others'. How the sight of a middle-aged man tickling a small girl in the plaza was amusing to everyone watching except me. I had come from a country where there are signs in playgrounds warning adults that they cannot enter unless accompanied by a child. In a place where physical, but not sexual, play is very much on the menu of daily life, I felt simultaneously fearful and guilty. I had come from a place where the starvation caused by the absence of Eros had squeezed through a crack in the collective psyche, had become the oozing corruption of paedophilia. Later I felt angry that we have grown so strange to ourselves that touching children is suspect. When the Rabbi Jesus told his friends to let the kids approach him, I have no doubt that he dandled them on his knee.

Ask the psychologists. For that matter, ask the zoologists about chimpanzees, rabbits, even bugs, for all I know. A child that cannot yet speak the language of its clan already knows the language of sensual touch. Without it, we shrivel and die. I fear that the contagion of curdled sensuality may make our children cold and unloving. When the estrangement from our own nature makes us dangerous to our own children, we need help from the older and less rational parts of ourselves, the places where Eros plays.

I hope it is clear by now that I am not advocating free love or any such nonsense. The last society that proposed that, the Soviet Union, became one of the most prudish countries in the world, with chaperones on every hotel landing. Control begets prudery begets repression begets perversion and violence. Nor am I asking for liberalisation of laws surrounding prostitution, though I can't honestly see what else we can do. I am asking us to open up our psyches a bit more in order to welcome back the other half of our humanity, which we have banished below stairs. Not just sexuality, but the kind of sensuality that makes us whole.

Nowadays, sensuality seems the unique domain of the young. All those beautiful young people whose images bombard us from television screens seem to exclude the rest of us from being sensually connected. But the contagion of repression is there as well; by eliminating all but explicit sexuality from the world of bodily sensation, we are left with but a poor, narrow channel. Eros in exile is dangerous.

You see, Eros is not the exclusive playmate of the young. He loves the lines and wrinkles on our faces, delights in our arthritic dance steps, lives on experience enriched by long memory. He is ready to go out and play whenever we are, at whatever age. The twinkle in the old man's eye, the flash of *duende* in the Spanish matron's glance, the rising of the ageing pulse to the rhythms of the eternal dance are meat and drink to him. He is the caller of the steps and the leader of the band.

Eros, as in his forest trysting place with Psyche, lives in the dark. We conspire in the maintenance of this darkness: we try to believe that what is unseen is non-existent. But each of has a lamp that can be lit to throw light upon a fearsome countenance that, surprisingly, closely resembles our own. When that is done, we resume the growth to which our souls are already committed and reclaim our destiny, which leads us home to ourselves. We will not get there by ignoring the sensual world that cradles us. We will not get where we need to go without having the will and courage to light the lamp.

Dealing with Dragons

If you live in England, you really ought to celebrate St. George's Day. We've all seen the images of St. George. There he sits astride his white horse, piercing the open mouth of the dragon. Who and what the dragon represents is a matter of debate. It is said that George came to the assistance of the crusaders at Antioch in the year 1098. In that case, the dragon must have represented the Islamic enemies of this most notorious excursion into imperialism. We share St. George with Portugal and with the Spanish province of Aragon, whose dragons might sometimes have been someone else—even ourselves. The usual interpretation of the symbol of the dragon is the Christian warrior's victory over evil, but just what constitutes evil in any one nation or epoch is anybody's guess.

At any rate, the case of St. George represents the classical method of dealing with a dragon. Armed with a sturdy lance of righteousness and valour, the Christian hero slays him. There are no questions asked and no quarter given: dragons are to be exterminated because they represent an obstacle to one's goal. They may be heathens propagating a false belief in one's personal God. They may be dark-hearted villains who have seized territory that one wishes for one's own. More than likely, there is a hidden motive at work: when the "savages" of North America, Australia, and Africa were defeated to bring European light to their darkness, one would certainly have seen the flag of St. George flying proudly and without self-doubt. Dragons are bad; we are good: "Go ahead, fire-breath, make my day."

Dragons come in many shapes and sizes. There was the Norse dragon, Grendel, who was actually half-human, who annoyed the king by killing his people in their sleep. Sleep is the time for dragons—ask any child. Beowulf didn't really want to know much about Grendel's ideas; he just wanted him dead.

The premier dragon of our Judeo-Christian tradition is Leviathan, the monster whom God exiled to the depths of the sea, thought to be a dangerous and forbidden place. This is probably why Orthodox Judaism forbids the eating of certain sea creatures, such as lobsters. Isaiah 27 states: *"This great and wide sea, wherein are things creeping, innumerable...there is that Leviathan, whom thou hast made to play therein."* What lies beneath the sea, the traditional symbol of the unconscious, is creepy; better to stay away from there.

But dragons are not always so clear cut. There are myths that shed a slightly different light on them. One I saw recently is a legend of the Nootka women of the Canadian Pacific Northwest, reported by Anne Cameron.[3] On a rocky seacoast, the trees have been stripped of their bark and twisted into strange shapes by the wind. It is believed that a monster named Sisiutl is to blame. He lives, like Grendel and Leviathan, under the sea, in the depths of the unconscious, and comes out unbidden from time to time to challenge the reason and order of the dry land. Sisiutl is a true monster. His form is like that of a snake, except that he has no tail. Where his tail should be is another head. Each head is more gruesome than the other; his breath is corruption and he brings terrible cold to the land.

If you are unfortunate enough to be on the shore when Sisiutl comes out, you may not survive it. Fixing you with eyes from both heads, he will come closer and closer, casting a spell of fear and paralysis over you. His intent is to devour you and chase your soul into the void, where you will forever weep in exile. People will sometimes hear your voice in the wind, but there is no help for you. That is what has happened to the deformed trees, you see: the bark has been sucked into the void, and only the strong roots keep the straining trunks from being pulled there also.

---

3. Anne Cameron, *Daughters of the Copper Woman*, The Woman's Press Ltd., 1984

Sisiutl is irresistible. As he comes closer, you are stricken with fear. It is all right to feel fear; you are human, after all. But you must not let your fear goad you into running, or he'll have you plucked off the earth and into the void. You must stand your ground, even when you see his terrible pairs of eyes and smell his foul breath. The fear cannot hurt you if you stand fast. When he is very near, he will curl himself around you. This is the most terrible moment of all, the time when all but the strongest struggle to escape the inescapable.

At that moment of deadly embrace, the two heads of Susiutl will see each other for the first time. And when each sees its opposite, something wonderful happens. The opposites merge and the monster finds wisdom. In his wisdom is gratitude toward you for being the agent of his realisation. In that moment, Sisiutl will bless you; this blessing is the blessing of wisdom, earned through overcoming fear.

To me, it is especially interesting that this is a story told by women. I say that because I have observed that women seem to deal with their personal dragons differently than men. It's as if the male qualities of military courage are less useful in dealing with this source of both destruction and blessing. If you kill Sisiutl, what you have is a dead reptile on the beach and a few stories to tell your friends. If you stand your ground, living through the fear, you will receive blessing. I have seen this blessing in many pairs of women's eyes—and in men's also—and I believe that their dragons have been seen off not with a sword, but with patience and the ability to bear pain in silence.

Sisiutl is rightly conceived as a two-headed monster. He is the monster of paradox, of the echo chamber of either/or that confronts us at every turn, splitting the unity of consciousness that is our birthright into a fragmented and unbalanced confusion. He is the dualism that separates soul from spirit, male from female, good from evil. And yet, for all his bad breath and fearsome eyes, we see that he is also our friend, the source of our blessing.

There is something about the story that almost makes you want to become a lone Native American woman on the windy shore, facing

Sisiutl. It almost seems a luxury to be able to identify your monsters so easily. Our own are more subtle, aren't they? Their names are alienation, addiction, denial. They appear not on the rocky shore, but in doctors' surgeries, midnight telephone calls, and cold courtrooms. Like Sisiutl, they threaten to whirl our souls into a void, to reduce us to spectres weeping in the wind, but we may not recognise them until it is too late.

We will do much, nearly anything, to avoid our dragons. We overlook them and surround ourselves with willing co-conspirators who will help us sustain the lies by which we live. We so numb ourselves with substances or obsessions that the dragons are nearly invisible. We take out insurance policies and practice magic rituals of diet and exercise to ward them off. If we are truly unsuccessful, we will keep them at bay all our lives, escape into history unscathed. We can slay them with self-improvement programmes and biofeedback, be like St. George, brave and victorious. But we must know, as the Nootka women know, that it is in an accepting encounter with Sisiutl that we find blessing.

We have all become adept at avoiding dragons. If it were possible, we would make danger illegal, as we increasingly try to do. We would outlaw viruses, identify potential paedophiles by DNA, control the weather. We would make ourselves live to a hundred and eighty and eliminate the species of *solanaceae* known as tobacco. There would be no high or deep places, and the world would become a park staffed by kindly rangers wearing Prozac smiles. We are trying to do all this even now.

But even then, perhaps in the world our children's children will inhabit, there will come an urge to go down to the beach, to the place where Sisiutl lives. The urge will be as ancient as the one to find safety. It will be the same one that makes people who have got it made eat of the fruit of the tree of good and evil, risking banishment. This urge is the same one that makes otherwise sane individuals go hang-gliding or rock climbing, the shadow side of which we can see in such activities as cigarette smoking or the practice of unsafe sex. It is the need to confront the uniquely human fate of knowing that one's existence is brief upon the earth and easily extinguished, and to live in that knowledge without shrinking.

People who have been down to the beach and dealt with Sisiutl have a certain look about them. I have known a few in my time, and so have you. It may be someone who has come through the cancer ward, not with the streaming banner of St. George, but with the soft gaze of someone who has found gratitude and peace. It may be in the eyes of an African refugee who has come out of his homeland injured and alone, but who has nevertheless stood his ground in the soul's moment of truth. It may be someone who has found calm water after a turbulent struggle with their sexuality, or someone who, as Oriah Mountain Dreamer has said, has had the courage to betray a trust in order to live truly.

The stony beach isn't all that far from here, you know. If you keep still for a moment—really still—and ignore the background chatter that is our mind's fragile refuge, you can just about hear the waves lapping the beach, the keening wind in the twisted trees. Yes, it is a fearsome place, because it is a place of truth. But is not a foreign place: each of us has known about it, whether we willingly admit it or not, all our lives. It is the half-glimpsed witch in the wardrobe of childhood, whom we have learned to ignore, but whom we will have to learn to embrace.

I don't know what lies in wait for you on that beach, but I think I do know what form Sisiutl may take for me. I'm getting myself ready now. I don't want to live halfway; that's not why I've come. I want my blessing, the one that has been waiting for me in the kind smile behind the dragon's teeth all along.

What is it Worth?

One of the first things you have to learn when trying to cope in a foreign language is that most basic question: "How much is this?" I suffered not long ago in Paris because of my bad French and then watched tolerantly in Spain as other foreigners did the same in Spanish. "How much is it?" seems to be the most frequently asked question, even more than "*Ou est le WC?*" This is because, at every turn in our market-oriented lives, everything has a price.

Some of us look at prices all day on computer screens and in pink newspapers. The rest of us wade through signs plastered in every shop window offering special sales and deals; without knowing it we become speakers of a new language that uses numbers as signposts to reality. I really believe that if you opened a shop in any city that had signs screaming: "Today—only 99p!" you would be flooded with customers, even if you didn't say what was for sale. That's because we are led by price, and our lives have become, as Wordsworth said, a matter of "getting and spending, late and soon."

Sometimes price is a relative thing. Mark Twain told the story of a man who arrives home, flushed with excitement, and tells his wife that he has sold their dog for a thousand dollars. "What?" she says, "That mangy old thing is worth a thousand dollars, fleas and all?" "Well," says her husband, "it wasn't exactly a cash sale. I traded him to a man for two cats, which he swears are worth five hundred dollars each."

All of us have probably got something like a five-hundred-dollar cat. When I was moving house recently I had to declare the value of my possessions for insurance purposes. In my peripatetic life I haven't acquired many possessions of "real" value. Not much furniture, art, silver cutlery, and so on. But I have got a few things that I would have to call priceless. There's a bird carved from a cow horn given to me by a Zambian friend a few weeks before he died; a Masai warrior's club that is a memento of a political struggle in Kenya that we lost, but lost well; a tapestry woven from a sugar sack and unravelled jumpers by someone named Sister Molefe. Those things might bring a few pence at a market stall down the Portobello Road, but they can't be considered valuable in the ordinary sense. When the hauliers wanted to know the replacement value, I realised there wasn't one. What something costs is not necessarily what it's worth. If you think about it, you've probably got the same priceless and worthless things at home.

We all survive a common crisis every four years. Wherever we may try to hide, we are all beset by news of that enduring orgy of competition, the Olympic Games. Stirring music, images of sweating, panting athletes, and chants of "higher, faster, better." If you didn't know better, you might think the games were a quadrennial event of McDonald's hamburgers and Nike shoes. At least on BBC One there's no overt advertising, but when I was in Spain the broadcasters used every opportunity to sell me cars and yoghurt and beer. The Olympics, too, are one big market.

Two thousand, five hundred years ago, Pythagoras made a similar observation. (Yes, the same guy who brought you the formula for the right-angled triangle's hypotenuse.) Pythagoras wasn't just a mathematician; he was the founder of a mystery school that used mathematics as a tool for understanding life. He once told his disciples that there were just three kinds of people, and that you could see them all at the Olympic Games.

First, there were those who came to buy and sell. When you get a lot of people together in one place, you get a market, and those whose lives are dominated by the love of gain will prosper, or try to. You can imagine the Greeks setting up their olive stalls or some such thing a couple of millennia ago. They're not so different from Coca-Cola and Sony as we might imagine.

There is something almost enviably simple about straightforward gain as a way of life. I know a man in Brighton like that. He grew up as a poor kid in East London, dropped out of school, and started making money. He used to sell "road kill" meat that he found on the highway at the back doors of cafes. Later on, he moved on to the grafting of money by "tarmacking" driveways—really only applying a coat of paint. Sometimes he would "repair" chimneys, too, after first giving them a few whacks with a six-pound hammer. He got enough together to buy a bed-and-breakfast hotel in Brighton, mortgaged to the hilt, and in a few years he sold it on and bought a bigger one. Now he owns a large seafront hotel and has lots of money. I would like to be able to tell you that his excessive materialism has made him miserable, but that's not the case. To all appearances, he's a happy man, generous and well-liked. He told me that he was always meant to be rich, and now he is.

I met him a few years ago in the bar of a yacht club, where I was a guest. When he found out what I did for a living, he was fascinated. He wanted to know what my "angle" was: did I get to keep the collection? I saw him the other day, and he was still bemused. I told him I had a vocation, or at least I thought I did, and he just smiled and shook his head. We have different ideas about what is important in life, but I admit that it's possible to envy him, even admire him a little. Pythagoras would recognise him at once.

The second of Pythagoras' types of people come to the Olympic Games to compete. This word has mixed meaning for us. We have made it a glorious concept in our market-driven world. We believe that competitive schools; competitive businesses, certainly; and even competitive hospitals are better. Some of us even think that churches should be competitive, but that's another chapter. We rarely stop to think that becoming a winner makes someone else a loser. That may be all right in track-and-field events, but it's a fairly tough model for life. You can appeal all you want to Darwin's theories, but losing out in terms of the necessities of life—as do the poor countries of the world when locked into an international marketplace—that is a hard game indeed.

Pythagoras identified the people who came to compete as those whose life values were based on honour. The olive wreath on the brow was the pinnacle of experience. You win or lose in the game of life based on the number of honours conferred upon you. If you have been a ruthless sugar baron, responsible for the deaths and suffering of millions, you can endow a series of libraries and art galleries, and rest—literally—on your laurels. It is almost as if those who began by seeking gain wind up craving something else, something they were formerly all too willing to forfeit—the admiration of others.

The third type of Pythagoras is a little different. He said that a few people come to the games not to buy and sell, nor to win. Remember the medal tally published every day in the newspapers? So many golds for China, so many bronzes for somebody else, with the good old USA, fatter and richer than the rest, up there on top? It is possible to compete vicariously, after all, and that is what most of us were doing, playing the honours game. The third type of person doesn't do this; they just come to observe, enjoy, and learn. Pythagoras called the goal of this third type the seeking of wisdom.

The ancient Greek philosophers meant something else than we may today when they spoke of wisdom. We may tend to confuse this word with intelligence, with education, even with the accumulation of information. But what they meant was much nearer to what we might call spirituality, or what the Buddhists know as enlightenment. The mind was a newish item for humanity in those days; they were exploring it as a means of connecting with the real, with God. So when Pythagoras or Socrates spoke of the search for wisdom, they were referring to the goal of all mystics and sages from the beginning. Enjoining us to search for wisdom was the same as saying, "Look in your heart for the truth."

If we look honestly at our lives, it isn't difficult to see the goblins of gain and honour peering through at us. Why, we say, only a fool completely ignores gain. That's true, isn't it? And who doesn't want honour, the respect and admiration of their friends, of their culture? Who doesn't feel a little bit better about themselves if everybody else admires them? So maybe we can admit the presence of the first two Pythagorean types without alarm. The question is, though, how much of us will remain for the seeking of wisdom?

The ancient Greeks were not so different from us. When people say that the Greek world is still the dominating model for our culture, they are not far off. There were a few—a very few—wise people around in those days, and they didn't always fare too well. Sometimes they had to drink a little hemlock tea or found themselves banished from Athens—a fate worse than death. But the voices can still be heard: the wit of Socrates, the dreaminess of Plato, the breadth of Aristotle. We know very little about the winners of races in those days, of whose brows the olive wreath rested on for a few moments. We know even less about the guys with the wine stalls who made a killing at the fairs. But the sweet breath of wisdom is still to be found from the groves where wisdom was sought and valued.

A few centuries later, Jesus added his voice. And, yes, we do have to listen to the young rabbi sometimes, whether we are Christian or not. He made no bones about what possessed value in life, making observations so familiar to us now that they have become clichés. "What does it profit you to gain the whole world and lose your own soul?" "What you sow is what you reap." And a fascinating line from Matthew 13, where Jesus is trying to explain to his friends what he means by the Kingdom of Heaven: "Like a merchant in search of fine pearls, who, on finding a pearl of great value, went and sold all that he had and bought it."

Being able to see through the tawdriness of marketplace life to the place of wisdom has a price. Jesus said that in order to find the treasure buried in a field, you had to sell what you have and buy the whole thing, the place where you know it is buried. As with the merchant, to get to the place of wisdom means abandoning everything else. I take this to mean that you can't seek wisdom while continuing the greedy pursuit of material possessions and attention. The pearl of great value is found when these other impulses are held in check. There's no more way to be a little bit wise than there is to be a little bit pregnant; that's what the pearl of wisdom costs, and it's very expensive. It is so expensive that, as in the later words of Meher Baba, "Everything—wealth, reputation, health, even life itself—must be sacrificed in the search for God."

Hard words, those. A high price indeed. There is very little scope for seeking wisdom in your spare time, being, shall we say, a weekend saint. It is not so much that you need all your energy for the real search, although I'm sure you do. It's more a matter of seeing the difference between the limited goals of wealth, honour, and all our other small obsessions and the only goal that really matters. If wisdom is what moves you, the other things become meaningless.

As always with the carefully-garnered words of the great ones, there is something strangely titillating about them, even though they spell the end of some of our favourite projects. And because none of us has had to live without the occasional glimpse of something more precious than money and fame, we know that the pearl of great value exists. Maybe we intuited it one morning when the mountain sunrise filled our minds with awe and wonder. Maybe at the end of a long dispute, we felt ourselves giving over our own narrow positions and felt peace flood into us. Maybe even looking into the open grave of a loved one, we felt the inexplicable "all-rightness" of things. In those moments, the pearl of great value, the wisdom of Pythagoras, was ours for a fleeting second, before the little people that we also are reasserted themselves, and distorted the world again.

Can we find a way into the third person, into the path of wisdom? What will it cost us to try? Can we afford it? Having seen it, however fleetingly, the question remains: can we afford not to?

How to Be Good

I have a friend who was sitting at home one afternoon when she heard a loud crash from the kitchen. She rushed in to find her five-year-old son standing white-faced beside an upturned and broken cookie jar. Before she could say anything, the boy cried out, "I didn't do it. The cat did it. I'll never do it again."

The boy had unknowingly recapitulated every ploy possible to get himself out of trouble: denying, blaming, and pleading for mercy. He got away with it because my friend burst out laughing, and it is very hard to punish someone if you're heaving with laughter. He was just too cute to punish. Maybe, too, my friend realised the truth of something Mark Twain said about morality: "We have no real morals, but only artificial ones, created and preserved by the forced suppression of natural and healthy instincts." The fact is, any of us might get caught with our hand in the cookie jar, whether that means fiddling an expense claim, getting lipstick on the collar, or something more serious, like, say, Watergate.

Social scientists who have studied morals have concluded that there is no perfect measure of virtues. A person who behaves well in some circumstances may behave badly in others. A television programme I watched recently revealed that the average person lies to someone twice a day. The same person may be a committed social activist or a passionate defender of the poor as easily as a cheque bouncer or peddler of pornography. The grab bag of human morality is as confused as we all are.

It seems that most thinkers have given up on the idea that moral values can be taught like algebra or basket-making. Socrates said a couple thousand years ago that, since he had never met anyone that could teach morality, it must be a divine dispensation. Studies have revealed that there is no obvious connection between the moral values of parents and children, so perhaps the other idea that morals rub off on you is not true either. We all know highly respected people with disreputable kids, and vice versa.

For one thing, we hardly know what to teach children. If we teach values like fair play, absolute truthfulness, and modesty, we may be hampering their chances in a competitive market-dominated world. If we teach values designed to help them get along with the society into which they were born, we may preclude the emergence of the kind of moral vision that has always characterised our heroes. By the same token, if we *show* them how we fudge our tax returns or lie to annoying relatives, they may internalise this hypocrisy and have a loose grip on the truth. If we try to live in an artificially high-minded way, the strained nature of our lives may turn them in an opposite direction. It seems that teaching and absorbing are not answers.

Society's view of morality and ethics usually stresses the desire for control. As Nietzsche sneered over a century ago, "Morality is the rationalisation of self-interest." Those mores and folkways come into being to keep some sort of order in the dealings of people with one another. Often they appeal to ideas emerging from scripture—especially the Bible. The so-called "Golden Rule"—doing unto to others as you would have them do unto you, has been exposed as a self-regarding ethic, because it's really about protecting yourself. It's the best way to be safe, but it bears little relation to being good.

Enter the conscience. Like the soul, this little item in human beings is hard to find, and even harder to understand. Psychopaths, we are told, don't have one. Hitler didn't either, though he wept at the sight of flowers and little girls' smiles. George Washington had a huge one, because he couldn't tell a lie, or so the propaganda goes where I grew up. We might imagine it as a kind of microchip set somewhere in the brain, a kind of default setting that makes most of us more or less okay.

Sigmund Freud, no respecter of bourgeois morality, identified it with the *superego*. This is something you acquire as you grow up, based upon the constant reinforcement of reward and punishment. It is about socialising a child into an agreeable entity by balancing the *ego* against the predatory, dark desires of the *id*. The superego is unglamorous in the extreme, bearing no relation to the jumbled codes we have inherited from religious teachings. It makes you feel guilt, that troublesome imp of modern humanity; it keeps you from going overboard, and very little else.

Another idea of the conscience comes from the deists, who included John Locke. Some of the deists, coming as they did during a new era of scientific idealism, saw the universe as a huge machine that God had built at the beginning of time. He had wound it up like a clock and left it to tick for aeons, until the end of time, when God came back to see how it all had gone. The conscience was built into people like a valve, and all people had to do was locate it and consult it from time to time.

This isn't far from the ideas of writer and business guru Charles Handy, who considers the conscience a kind of gyroscope that tells a pilot in the fog whether his plane is upright or not. There is an inbuilt sense of right and wrong in us, according to him, and its *modus operandi* is its connection with God. Unlike the deists, Handy and most contemporary churchmen believe that God is an active player in the working out of the universe, not a remote clock winder. His metaphor is appropriate, because in present times we are all flying in the fog.

A few decades ago, the school of *situational ethics* came into being. This arose partly out of the stern vision of existentialists like Jean Paul Sartre, who held that no present moral case bears any relationship to the past. Each new encounter with the world arrives without rules, and it is dependent upon the good faith of the individual to respond in an authentic way. The situational-ethics proponents drew upon certain statements of Jesus, who broke Hebraic law with the intention of "fulfilling the law." Situational ethics denies the possibility of any absolute morality and substitutes instead an open approach to the "spirit" of the law.

By the time that Marx and Engels got going, morality had taken a whole new turn. The phrase "The end justifies the means" became a cynical rationalisation for self-interested behaviour, because the outcome is impossible to envisage. The subjection of history to the fantasies of a few radical schemers is an invitation to mayhem, and so it has proven so far. It's all too easy to imagine that the world would be better off without some troublesome nation or ethnic group, or that making an investment in a corrupt regime is the same thing as helping the poor.

It may seem that the whole landscape of morality and ethics is nothing but a dense jungle of ideas. You can't teach it, and you can't seem to catch it. It's not necessarily a part of your equipment when you come into the world, so you can't rely on a valve or microchip. You can't memorise rules, because they are made to be broken, or at least reinterpreted in changing situations. The Golden Rule is showing some green around the edges, and the cynical voice of old cigar-puffing Sigmund can be heard over all, turning everything into a psychological pudding. So how do we learn how to treat each other, now that the buffalo's gone? How do we sort out right from wrong?

As with most complex problems, there is no clear answer. That is, there is no way to address such a convoluted problem simply by subjecting it to the echo chamber of the mind. As the song says, it's a gift to be simple. Some things may need the treatment of philosophical high-flyers, but it's possible to look at human morality in another way. You may not be able to puzzle your way out of the moral maze; you may have to learn to trust your feelings. Morality contorts the mind but finds a safe harbour in the heart. Doing good is not so much an idea as a feeling.

To understand morality in this way, you have to turn to those whose paths led them to experience ultimate reality, not just theorise about it. Of course I'm talking about the mystics of all traditions, East and West: Hindu, Muslim, Christian, Jew, and nothing at all. With what must be considered a single voice, we are told that, as Meher Baba said, "You and I are not we but one." It is a simple but startling statement. The separateness that we feel is not what we truly are. In some way, on some day we have yet to experience, all will be known as one being, who is most often called God. Here's how Julian of Norwich put it in the fifteenth century: "Our soul is oned to God, unchangeable goodness, and therefore between God and our soul there is neither wrath nor forgiveness, because there is no between." Between, according to the saint, implies two distinct beings.

In however many traditions you care to name you will find this idea expressed over and over again. When the threshold of the truth is reached, you find there not the seat of the ultimate other, but that of your own true self. This oneness is the reason, say the great ones, that love exists. Love is a kind of preview, or intuition, of the experience of oneness. It might be mixed with passion, a sense of belonging to a family, the affection for a friend or an animal; it might be many things, but what it really is, is oneness seen, as it were, through a glass darkly.

That's why it has so often been said that God is not a noun but a verb; when you get near to understanding, you may experience something *godding*. The awareness is not quite there—you can't quite put your finger on it—but it is a taste of true identity, oneness manifesting as love.

Many of the great saints have described their experiences of feeling for others. Francis of Assisi, for instance, focussed on lepers. They talk about feeling the pain of others, of experiencing it nearly as directly as their own. They are aware of the oneness of things. Our own sense of human sympathy is a version of the same thing—a preview of oneness that we cannot yet experience fully.

What this means is that morality is not a code, a rulebook, or a user's manual. It is a sense, like the other senses but one that can perceive facts only dimly and distantly. When you are treating others with kindness, in some way you are treating yourself with kindness. When you are not cheating, stealing, killing others, it is because they are, in some dimly-perceived but no-less-actual sense, yourself. After all, Jesus didn't say "Love your neighbours as much as you love yourself." What he said was, "Love your neighbour *as yourself.*"

The key to morality is not learning as much as it is forgetting. Forgetting the tangle of ethical codes in favour of feeling for others. Forgetting the differences we put between us, because, as Julian tells is, there *is* no between. Forgetting the false picture of ourselves we have cultivated from the cradle. Forgetting to take advantage, forgetting to despise. I believe that the truth of that ultimate oneness finds ways to leak through the billowing curtain of our little lives, and sometimes, like a stray sunbeam, lights up our hearts.

The Trouble with Sandcastles

Did you ever build a sandcastle? All that joyful, sweaty work that went on for hours, while your shoulders turned red and your mother pleaded with you to put on sun cream. Turrets and drawbridges, little flags made of sweet wrappers. And then your feelings as the tide inexorably swept in, lapped at the moat, eroded the walls, and finally turned all your work into what you started with. Try to remember what your feelings were as the castle disappeared into the sea. Were you frustrated, sad, excited? Did it fill you with resolve that next time you would make walls to protect it or build it farther up the beach? Or did it leave you feeling that it hadn't been worth it after all?

The philosopher Friedrich Nietzsche is reported to have said that people could be divided into three types: those who build sandcastles, oblivious to their inevitable end; those who, knowing that sandcastles don't last, simply avoid building them; and, finally, those who know that they are only temporary but build them anyway.

The metaphor is obvious: some of us are reckless or wilfully blind to truth and go on trying to build something of permanence in a world of change. Maybe we are all like that when we are young, and the sad stories of the rise and fall of civilisations hasn't occurred to us—history is just something we have to study at school. Some of us change as we age, but some of us just seem to keep trying for immortality, practising denial, one might say.

Then there are those whose experience of the encroaching tides overwhelms them. This is perhaps a version of depression, when all that is left to say is that ancient refrain: "What's the use?" Why build sandcastles, why engage in any sort of activity knowing that it is all ultimately doomed to failure anyway? Take a look at yourself and ask if you have never had this bleak vision afflict you. There are some among us who are so poisoned by this view that suicide becomes the logical thing to do. There but for the grace of God, you might well say.

It is the third of Nietzsche's types that interests me. Knowing that life and its hopes are fleeting, the third person engages with it anyway. What kind of person is this? First, there are overtones of the hedonist motto, "Eat, drink and be merry, for tomorrow we die." In this worldview, the acquisition of pleasure and the avoidance of pain are the most important things. As in Plato's metaphor, the hedonist uses what is called the "argument of the leaky jug." The person is a jug with a hole in the bottom. Liquid that escapes through the leak is pain; liquid that enters through the top is pleasure. The trick in life is to make pleasure outweigh pain. Socrates' response was to differentiate between what is called pleasure and what is called happiness; it seems that they are not the same thing at all. If you consult your inner oracles, I think that you'll find that one can be happy without much of what is called pleasure. In fact, you could even say that happiness begins where pleasure ends.

Also among Nietzsche's happy beach architects might be those who believe that the *now* is everything. These would include Zen Buddhists, Taoists, and even a few stoics thrown in for good measure. Knowing that life and its projects are perishable, one engages with the *eternal now*, which is the point, as Meher Baba said, "where time touches eternity." This is a lofty idea, and much effort is expended in its practice through the sitting of *zazen*, yoga exercises, and various other forms of meditation. It is an ideal for me, and every time I read Thich Nhat Hanh I vow I'm going to work on this. The problem is, it seems to me, that even when I have had timeless instants, felt in touch with eternity, the next moment is always on its heels. Monday keeps coming around, full of its own opportunities for ruin and salvation; the more I hurry, the farther behind I seem to get.

We can stay there if you like, in the present, on the beach engaged in the search for the *eternal now*. But something seems to be pulling me further along. You can go with me if you wish, but if you have found your own reasons to keep on building sandcastles you can stay here—it's a good place to be. I'd like to think I could escape from time into the *eternal now*, but I keep getting yanked back; I can feel the surf coming in my bones, and the stop-frame solution doesn't make me feel safe.

I seem to need to embrace the washing away of my castle. I seem to need to find in its hard truth some way to recognise the ephemeral nature of my life without yielding to despair. And I need to find a way not to resent the cruel working of change but to give it my active and even joyful support.

Recently I engaged in an important conversation with Socrates. Not the old guy who drank hemlock, but someone else who knew how to ask me a question that cut right to the heart of my theology. That person may not have known that they were being Socratic in their method and may not have taken my response to heart. I don't know. I'll tell you the story anyway.

I was performing a house visit with an elderly member of the church. It was a routine visit, but I was also there to collect material for a funeral service, if that became necessary. But we didn't talk about that at all. We sat around and ate Viennese pastries and drank coffee and laughed and told stories all afternoon. It began to get dark, and I rose to leave. I was standing by my chair when my friend said, "I suppose there is one question I should ask you: do you believe in life after death?"

You might be surprised to hear that we Unitarian ministers seldom hear this most important of all life's questions. This is the BIG ONE that is probably too big to ask. We must assume that people think that no one knows, and so why ask? But this one took me by surprise, and before I had time to think, I heard myself saying this: "Yes, I do. And I think we're already living it."

It was as if a million little tumblers had fallen together in some lock of my mind and the door had swung open on smoothly oiled hinges. I think we were both startled for a second, and then I started to explain, as much to myself as to my friend: I believe that who we really are has always existed, before our birth, during our life span, and after we die. I think the reason we don't realise it while we live is because we are too busy being merely ourselves to feel being everybody and everything, which is what we truly are. I think that that is the reason for prayer and meditation and poetry: it puts us just that little bit in touch with our real selves. I think it is the only valid reason for what is called ethics and morality—doing harm to others is doing harm to one's true self. I think people like Jesus and Buddha and Milarepa remind us of our true selves, and this is why we deify them. And I think that what we call love is a visible sign of that invisible reality: loving is feeling the underlying oneness of things.

I don't know about you, but I have never felt comforted by what I think of as the "recycling" theology. That is the idea that when we die we release our elements—all those lovely things that formed our eyelashes and tonsils and warm beating hearts—to become leaves and spider webs and plastic yo-yo's. I don't mean to demean this idea, because it has provided comfort to many. But I guess I don't think that I am solely my molecules; I think I am the consciousness that organises all of that, and what happens to that?

A few days later I was standing by a grave in Highgate Cemetery, and I read these ancient words: "Earth to earth, ashes to ashes, dust to dust." I also said, "Take back, creation, your child; reweave her into the fabric of the universe." I think I might have added, if I had thought to, "soul to soul" alongside "dust to dust."

Let's leave these elevated surroundings and go back to the beach for a moment. What about our sandcastle? How does all this help against the predation of the waves?

Fritz Perls, founder of Gestalt psychology, made an interesting observation. In trying to decipher dreams he left behind the old notion of Freud that dreams are merely cryptic reproductions of the issues of the unconscious psyche. Perls made the point that if you dream, say, about being on a train with a pretty woman, you are not only yourself in the dream, but also the pretty girl, and even the train on which you are riding. In other words, you are not just the main character, but all the minor ones as well, and you are not just the hero, but you are the whole dream. To apply this to sandcastles, you are not only the castle, though that is where you have put your focus, you are also the sand and the sea itself: that is who you really are.

The grains of sand are redistributed by the waves. They don't disappear. What disappears, or appears to disappear, is a fleeting form, a pattern of the grains of sand. You organised it, and the "larger you" redistributed it, just as your life is organised and then redistributed. Nothing is lost; everything changes.

But this pattern: where did *it* go? The teacher Meher Baba once pointed to an explanation of this when he made the observation that all projects—including the project of what we call a human life—are not the point. All these things are simply scaffolding to enable work on an invisible project. After the invisible project is complete, the scaffolding is dismantled. And then reused somewhere else. That is the real sense underlying the "recycling" theory of life: the base materials, the grains of sand or the molecules of the body must be reused, but the invisible project remains.

And this invisible project? Where is it? A clue comes from some words I read at the same funeral last week from Kahlil Gibran, and I have reason to know that you have heard them before: "You shall be together, even when the white wings of death scatter your days. You shall be together…in the silent memory of God…" The silent memory is silent because it is invisible to our gross eyes and indecipherable to our gross minds. What Gibran means by the term "God" you are free to interpolate. For myself, I would say something like this: "Everything in every direction forever, and the consciousness that organises it."

You never know when something like a sandcastle is going to lead you on to reflections about life, the universe, and everything. What remains for me is the wise Socratic question my friend asked that afternoon, and my feeling that the life before and after death is with us now, if we could only just remember it. But you never know when the veil of forgetfulness will part for an instant and let you gaze with clear eyes at the sea of deep meaning, not just at our small projects on the shore. And if it doesn't happen so often, well, we can count on being in touch with it when the tide does its magic and takes the grains of sand back into itself. In the meantime, let's encourage each other, keep wondering, and, through it all, enjoy.

There are hundreds of lovely sandcastles still waiting to be built.

Trout Tickling for God

Have you ever tickled a trout? I have tried, but I've never caught one. Here's how you do it. Lie on a flat stone in a trout stream and dangle your arms in the water. Try not to wriggle around, even though it's probably cold, and don't disturb the bottom if you can help it. At first, the water will be hard to see through. That's because of all the reflected light on the surface, but after a while your eyes will adjust and you'll be able to see quite clearly.

The next part is tricky, because it involves a process of—to steal a phrase from the Buddhists—*unlearning*. All your life you have been learning to search for things, to maintain your vision in a state of tight focus. To tickle a trout you need to relax your eyes, let the emphasis on focus gently become a process of gazing, as you do when you let your eyes rest on the far distance. At first you won't see anything much, but then, you're not peering; you're trying to see without effort. After a few moments, the landscape at the bottom of the stream will start to appear more clearly. Resist the urge to focus; just relax and wait.

You will suddenly see a trout. The fish will be quite visible, but before you will have seen nothing of it. Then others: you will note that dark-topped fish hug the shadows and hover above dark stones; light-hued fish will seek the bright sands. This is their strategy for hunting and for protection, a subtle camouflage that works on prey as well as predators. If you have been still, sooner or later a trout will actually nudge your hand, and if you are quick—and perhaps hungry—you'll have him. Just like that.

The process of unfocussing on the particular is like seeing the forest suddenly appear among the trees. Have you ever noticed what happens to children's art when they reach the age of, say, six? What used to be a tangle of lines and colours suddenly becomes intelligible. You start getting a strip of blue at the top—that's the sky; and a strip of green at the bottom—that's the grass. What emerges is more accurate, perhaps, but what has happened is that the child has stopped seeing and begun thinking. It's a great day for their future careers, but a bad one in terms of seeing reality. The art of direct apprehension fades to admit the skill of interpretation.

I believe that seeing through the apparent world we inhabit is something like that. If you want to reconnect (that's a definition of *religion*, by the way; from the Latin root words of *re* and *ligare*) with the life that we don't just live, but actually *are*, it's necessary to start seeing clearly again. Not peering frantically for explanations, but gazing receptively at that for which explanations are a poor substitute—*meaning*.

There are a number of time-tested ways to do this. You can sit in *zazen* meditation, practise yoga, do a sacred dance like the dervish, or pray without ceasing. In all these techniques, discipline is required, and that discipline can only be motivated by the faith that, having transcended the merely apparent, you can encounter the real.

But many of us aren't like that. The veil of the ordinary obscures our sight, and, worse, makes us doubt that there is anything else to see. What we need we sometimes find by accident: a glimpse of a dew-bedecked mountain landscape, perhaps, or the smile of a newborn infant, which may grant us a glimpse of that reality behind the apparent—a mystical experience, if you like. But these are soon covered by the same veneer of illusory perception, this time in the form of memory. What we need is a new way of walking through our days, a way of gazing into life the way the trout tickler gazes into the stream. We need to unfocus our probing, scheming vision and begin to see with what a friend of mine calls the "gaze of completion."

With this form of seeing, you are not escaping from the world into some promised land, into the "sweet by and by" of the fundamentalists. You are not escaping at all. In fact, you are engaging with the world in a much deeper way. You are preparing to see in a stone or a leaf, as Thomas Wolfe did, the "lost lane end into heaven." You are preparing to engage with senselessness until it reveals the order of eternity. You are preparing to find in one life, all life—the life that we are.

We can learn this art the way the trout tickler does. There is nothing complicated about it except the complications with which we burden it. If you walk cheerfully, as George Fox said, "greeting that of God in everybody"—and I add, "everything"—you are going to meet it. That's not conjecture. That's a fact. The life that we have lived before birth, during life, and after death is not less real than this one of surfaces and reflections. It is realer than this one, because this one depends upon it. If you don't believe me, ask Jesus, ask St Teresa, ask Rumi.

So, I tell myself, don't search, because your hard peering makes you nearsighted. Don't analyse, because the logic of the marketplace isn't up to the knowing of eternity. Gaze gently, expecting to see the real, and—I believe—in time you will.

Feeding Your Angel

Here's some bad news: angels are out of fashion. It is true that they make periodic comebacks in John Travolta films and on television, but there they seem to have no more reality than monstrous aliens in the *X-Files* or werewolves in old black-and-white movies. They dropped out of sight in all but the most conservative of theologies a century ago, victims of the ambitions of reason on the sanctity of myth. Now they occupy a place of indifferent exile alongside fairies, leprechauns, and the old Greek gods.

But lately, new prospectors have been scratching about in these abandoned mines of meaning. Angels may not be winged beings that carry away the saintly or who fire arrows into the hearts of lovers, but they may have an unexpected persistence about them, one that we can't afford to ignore.

My dictionary gives two definitions of angel in addition to the obvious one of the winged harp player: "an attendant spirit or guardian" and a "messenger or harbinger." The first suggests the lovely spirit that is said to watch over drunks, idiots, and children, the guardian angel of fantasy fiction. The second is that creature perched on the foot of the deathbed or the messenger who told Mary that she was to give birth to Jesus. These creatures we may be able to dispose of with the cool light of our hard-won cynicism, but in this case, as in so many others, we have to ask the question: "Are we throwing the baby out with the bath water?" or "Are we consigning something to the archives of childhood that belongs in the active present?"

In recent years, one of the most persistent diggers in this abandoned mine has been James Hillman, the depth psychologist and founder of "archetypal analysis." He is a post-modern Jungian philosopher in the "transpersonal" realm who, along with many others, has augmented C. G. Jung's theory that at the core of our individual psyche there is a universal existence. That is, at a certain point of resolution, our individual lives and histories open onto a collective form of being that is universal. This is so close to many Eastern theologies as to be obvious, but Jung seems to have arrived at the idea not through divine revelation of sacred texts, but through the investigation of human minds, including his own. Jung used the figures of the ancient gods of all traditions to speak of certain basic patterns, or archetypes, that lie within us all. These are not real beings, but building blocks of personality. They include such figures as Apollo, Dionysus, and Persephone and represent real elements of the human psyche: they exist in us.

And so no one, least of all Jung, believes any more that these are real gods with houses and gardens somewhere in the clouds above Mt. Olympus. Nor, as the equivalent gods of the Tswana people of Southern Africa, do they live in caves in the mountains, nor in Valhalla with Thor and Odin, nor in the sea off Tahiti. But the very fact that these figures are universal in their mythic appearance indicates that they have at least a figurative existence in the human psyche. No wonder that they became gods to the ancients. And no wonder, says James Hillman, that a certain ineluctable human experience of divine guidance became a winged creature called *angel.*

In his book, *The Soul's Code,*[4] Hillman advances a theory of human personality that builds upon the theory of archetypes. What concerns him is the ancient questions of human identity: *Who am I? Why am I like I am? What does it mean?*

He intervenes in an argument about human nature that has dominated the physical and social sciences for decades: *nature versus nurture.* One side insists that we are mostly controlled by genetics, not just in eye colour or susceptibility to diabetes, but also in personality. The advocates of this theory confidently predict that in time bio-chemical

---

4. James Hillman, *The Soul's Code: In Search of Character and Calling,* Time Warner Bookmark, New York, NY, 2003

geneticists will find genes to explain nearly everything about a person, from her philosophy of life down to her favourite colour socks. In several recent cases, advocates of this genetic determinism have been accused of racism and worse.

On the other side, advocates of the "nurture" theory say that what happens in early life determines the shape of the personality. Environment shapes the person, and entire theories of therapy have evolved since Freud with this single constant in mind. It must be *nurture*, not *nature*, they argue, because there are cases of twins who enter the world with nearly identical genetic codes who vary greatly in their outcomes. The nature types are fascist, they claim sometimes, because you can't tell from a blood test who will be a criminal and who a humanitarian. This opens Pandora's Box (she was created by our old friend Hephaestus, by the way) to a scary world of eugenics presaged by the Nazis. And it has equally frightening consequences for us now, in a new age of "designer babies."

Hillman urges a third way. Not denying that both genes and environment are significant in shaping the personality, he argues that there is yet another element in the equation. This he refers to as the *daemon*, or the *genius*, or, more familiarly, the *angel*. This angel bears a close resemblance to the old guardian of legend and fiction: it is personal, it is invisible, and it has the desire to protect. The departure from these older forms comes in the way it wants to protect. Its job is not to keep you from getting knocked down by a bus in the street, but to help you follow the destiny or karma that your soul needs in order to grow. Where it came from and what it means theologically are separate questions. If you interpret this to mean that you will be reincarnated, fine. If you take it to imply that our time on earth is *about something*, and not just a cosmic accident, that is all right, too.

The great musician Yehudi Menuhin, Hillman tells us, was born knowing what he had to do. At the age of three he asked for a violin for his birthday. When the day finally came and he saw that what he had been given was a toy instrument with wire strings, he smashed it in a rage. Within months he was playing on a real one, and the rest is history. But the angel is not always so accommodating. In the case of the artist Gauguin, the daemon sent him to the South Sea Islands, destroying him and his family in the process but leaving behind some wonderful works of art.

Hillman has compiled a number of such stories, some of the famous and some of us more ordinary mortals. A single theme runs through them all, which Hillman has taken as the keystone of his psychotherapeutic method: we are all born with certain purposes in place; they represent the basis of who we are. That is, we all have an angel, whose job it is to keep us on track with our soul's work in the world.

It may be difficult to conceive that we have such a guiding spirit. In the rough-and-tumble confusion of ordinary life, it is hard enough just to pay the rent without indulging in fantasies of soul quests. And besides, we are just ordinary people, not artists or saints or violinists. What meaning could that theory have for us?

Hillman would answer that not all angels are calling us to found religious orders or play in the Albert Hall. Most angels are ordinary, just as we are ordinary, and they have ordinary things in store for us. Sometimes—often, in fact—these buried goals are neither profitable nor "sensible." They might, if they were heeded, lead us away from financial success or social approval. One might feel that being a minister is "right," while the angel insists upon the person becoming a bartender. The staid insurance man, such as Wallace Stevens, might incredibly become a poet. The world is full of stories of people who made enormous shifts in life, and whether or not they became rich and admired, they very often became *happy*.

It is happiness, above all, that is at stake. I don't mean fun, or pleasure, or even comfort, because none of that is material to the angel. Happiness is something else, something that comes from being in step with one's true design and living that design as fully as possible. Happiness can include sorrow, pain, loneliness, and isolation—in fact, it eats these things for breakfast—because happiness is about meaning, that thing in the name of which wars are fought, fortunes squandered, and lives ruined. And as hard as its appearance might seem to us, to live without a chance of it is hardly to live at all.

The angel is serious about his work. If you stray too far from the basic pattern of your soul's life, suggests Hillman, you'll probably get sick. Most psychological illnesses and depressions stem from a lack of meaning. The practitioners of existential analysis know this all too well. According to one of their founders, Viktor Frankl, it is possible to be happy in a concentration camp—he was. Not comfortable, not full of pleasure, not without fear and pain, but *happy*. That was the work of his angel, who kept him to his task until he became a great healer. We may not have nearly to starve and be worked to death to serve our angels, but Viktor did. The angel doesn't mess around.

Our angel comes without a user's manual. He or she or it isn't a pet bird in a cage, but it does require feeding. And how does one feed one's angel? Here are some suggestions:

Listen to it. When you are depressed or ill without apparent cause, your angel is probably trying to speak to you. Hillman hints that the direction of our "pathologising" is the direction of our growth. Our symptoms often inform us. Recently I had a problem with my hip joint. I began to think of replacement operations and so on—one day I probably will need that. But a friend asked me, "Have you been wrestling with any angels lately?" And it came to me that Jacob had dislocated his hip when he was trying to find a new home.

The angel said to him, "Release me."

Jacob replied, "I will not release you until you have blessed me." And mine did. I can't tell you how—that *is* too personal. But I can say that it made all the difference.

Listen to your pain, but also listen to your joy. Try to notice in those rare moments when the world seems a kind and beautiful place what has caused the experience. Is it because of a connection to some beautiful natural place, the soulful sounds of some music, a glimpse of a half-forgotten face? Take your angel out with you; give him or her or it a chance to see the world and its infinite possibilities. If you suddenly swell with joy in front of a shoe store, maybe you want to dance. If it's luggage, the pilgrim within might want to take you on an odyssey. Go looking, go listening; the world is full of clues.

If you know something of your soul's lost direction, turn towards it. It's a little like that parlour game "hot and cold"—when you're getting near the lost object, you're getting warmer. When you turn away from it, whether through cowardice or sloth or lack of attention, things get colder, and you get more lost and sick.

One last thing: take your angel along with you. Others would like to get to know it, too. It might help us help each other, take away all that clutching need for sameness that holds us back. One day we might organise a party for all our angels. How would that be? We could have angel's food cake. In the meantime, let's be alert for the faint whisper of wing beats. I'll listen for yours and you listen for mine.

Welcome to the Lens Grinder's Shop

Do you wear reading glasses? Remember when you first had to put them on? For me it came after two years in Africa. When I got back I was staying in Birmingham and noticed I had bad headaches at bedtime. It also tired me out to read for long. So I went to the optometrist in the high street for an eye test. It was an interesting half-hour. I learned three things. One, there is about 40% less ambient light in the UK than in sub-Saharan Africa. Two, the eyes use about a quarter of the body's calories, which is why in those sad pictures of Ethiopian famine the kids all seem to have a fixed expression: they just can't afford the energy it takes to look around. And three, oh yes, I was getting old and needing reading glasses.

Getting over the shock of this first sign of mortality, I became interested in lenses. I used to try on other people's to see how they worked and was amazed to find how differently we see. The differences are mostly the result of what is called "focal length," how we filter and adjust light. If somebody with really poor eyesight loses their glasses, things don't just become blurry; they all but disappear in a haze of pure light. Everything we see is just patterns of light made comprehensible by focussing it through a lens—both the lens of the biological cornea and that of our spectacles.

You can take that idea and extend it. We are told by physicists that everything in the universe is composed of energy in various forms. When it's moving a lot, it's pure energy, the most visible form of which is light. When it's slowed down a little, it's what we call matter. That's a crude version of their ideas, but it will serve for the purposes of the metaphor. What this means is that everything we see and feel in the world—all the trees, sand dollars, bird's eggs, hot dogs, and fish ponds—are concentrations of this energy. They exist for us because we have the sensory organs to perceive them. They are our reality, but the reality is contingent upon our ability to detect them. Some geniuses may speak about other forms of matter that we can't perceive, things way out there in space, but we'll leave them to sort that out.

Let's stay with the image of the lens for a moment. One way to look at the ultimate reality, that which we call God, is as an infinite cloud of energy, or light. Some of the language of Hindu mysticism, very close in some amazing ways to quantum physics, describes Atman in just this way. No one has seen this reality face to face; there's always something like a burning bush acting as an interface. But people have always tried to focus from their own vantage points on this transcendent reality. You might say that they have evolved cultural lenses to focus the one eternal light.

The lens you use is formed by the culture into which you were born. If you are a pre-literate inhabitant of the ancient world, you look at the canopy of stars by night and see things that make sense to you: a giant bear, an archer or a ram, for example. All these things exist in your world. They are familiar, and so God or the gods look like a part of your reality. Apollo drives a fiery chariot across the sky; the sun is not an ongoing nuclear explosion with temperatures of 140 million degrees centigrade. What you see is what you know; the lens is specific to your time and place.

The philosopher Michel Foucault spoke about what he called the "discourses," which are a kind of philosophical lens. A discourse is a kind of story, as systems of mythology are. He described the modern examples of this, saying that the Marxist discourse was complete and logic-tight. You can explain anything in terms of class struggle if you want. The same goes for Freudian psychology, with its deterministic theories of human consciousness. And we mustn't leave out Charles Darwin, whose theory of evolution created a discourse that has spilt over its container and become a theory of human society, not just an explanation of all those television wildlife programmes.

Foucault always denied that he was a philosopher. He called himself an "archaeologist." What interested him was not whether a certain theory was right or wrong, but why people believed it. In other words, he was a collector of the stories we humans have lived by through the millennia. If you occupy a certain story or outlook on reality, it becomes real.

A friend of mine named Phred was once moved to pity by the sight of some Easter chicks being sold at a fair. You know, little one-day-old creatures died pink and green and sold to children. He bought all the vendor had and tried to keep them alive, but only two survived. When they were old enough he put them with some laying hens in a coop. The problem was, one of these was a baby duck, not a chicken. A mix-up at the hatchery, I guess. Anyway, the duck grew up believing it was a chicken. When I saw them, they were a year or so old. They were inseparable, but they had to make some adjustments. The chicken had talons and liked to roost off the ground. The duck had these little webbed feet and so would wobble on its perch until it learned to grip somehow.

One day they followed us down to the river to a little swimming hole. The duck was moved by instincts it had never felt before. It went over to the pond and suddenly was in it, splashing and paddling like a pro. The chicken went mad, squawking and flapping its wings. The duck, perhaps feeling low self-esteem from being such a lousy chicken, got out of the water and resumed scratching in the ground alongside the chicken. But then its instincts got the better of it and it went for another swim and ate worms or some such thing happily out of the mud. It was very funny, but I did feel pity for the duck; he was a prisoner of his story, and just couldn't get far enough out of it to help himself.

A few thousand years ago, the stories people lived in were different. At the time of Zoroaster, an epoch of much war and destruction, people saw God as having an enemy. This made sense, because who didn't? Their story was one about Ahurumazda, the universal force of good, and Ahriman, the force of evil. The struggle between these two forces was reflected not just in the way people worshipped, but the way they lived. The lens of the day, the way the universal light was focussed, had shaped their story.

When the Buddha came along, Hinduism had already paved the way. The world was an illusion, a complicated dance performed by Maya. The illusion was very strong, and so the way forward was to transcend it altogether, not just progress toward perfection, as Rama had taught. The story of the early Buddhist was the escape from the wheel of births and deaths through a kind of refusal to participate in the dance. This was accomplished through self-abnegation, meditation, and the practice of compassion. The goal was Nirvana, a state of non-existence that represented total liberation. This lens suited the agrarian, riverside cultures of Asia very well, and it focussed the lifestyle and religious efforts of the people.

Jesus appeared at a time when the Hebrew world had been rocked by the events of the Maccabean war against the Greeks, when thousands of their young men had been killed, apparently contrary to the promises of Jehovah. What is worse, they were a subject state of the Roman Empire, ruled over by a puppet king from, of all places, Samaria, the low-rent district of the Jewish world. Jesus extended the ideas of the sect known as Pharisees, which promised a world after this one. Heaven was a new idea to Judaism. With his insistence on a loving father rather than a stern king for a God, the charismatic rabbi focussed the chaotic light of changing times into a new story, one which affects us still.

Each epoch has had its story and its lens with which to focus the light of reality, or God. Human beings demand lenses with which to make sense of the world, and they can be protective about them. Wars are still fought because two cultural lenses focus the light differently.

You don't have to go farther than the Balkans to see that. Or, for that matter, Northern Ireland.

The thing is, lenses are only useful for a while. The light changes, the world turns, and you find yourself squinting through lenses that are worn out. In my case, my reading glasses are getting a little stronger every few years. I only know it when I get a headache in front of the computer and find that I'm really not seeing very well.

Religious lenses, the means by which you focus the light of God, are just the same. What made sense in a former generation just doesn't work a little later. The stories shift, through events like World War I and the publication of Einstein's theory of relativity. The lenses we inherit just don't do the job for us, and we get spiritual eyestrain or even go blind.

There have been times in my life when certain religious lenses seemed, for a season, to work. I'm old enough to have been brought up in a more or less intact Christian culture. I'm speaking of the American South and its unsophisticated charm. I have been able to wear the Christian lenses, perhaps not with perfect comfort, but without terrible headaches. Sometime in my adolescence, I don't know exactly when, I needed a change of prescription. Later on, in my twenties, psychedelic substances and Eastern mysticism became the means by which I focussed the light. Then things changed again. So I put away my Herman Hesse and Alan Watts books and read E. F. Schumacher and Paolo Freire. My need for lenses changes all the time, as my vision does, even if the one light remains the same.

I believe that we have used up our inherited lenses. Trying to peer through our granddad's spectacles is inefficient and painful. How he focussed the light with them suited his time, not ours. We need new pairs of our own if we want to see clearly again.

And I don't suggest we need to go around switching lenses all the time. Put on a pair of Sufi ones today, Christian mystical ones tomorrow, and Buddhist ones next week, and you are engaging in mere eclecticism, and it will just make you dizzy. What I think we need to do is grind our own, take the pain and fear of our life and use it as an abrasive to grind the glass, then take the joy and love that is also ours and use its softness to polish the lens clear. I don't think we can become a spiritual Bausch and Lomb and pass out standard prescriptions. Even worse, we don't want to be in the business of marketing trendy sunglasses that make everything look rosy. I don't think we can manufacture any lens at all. What we can do is to help each other grind our own, until we are all able to see clearly. You help me; I'll help you.

The reason I think we can do that is that I think we are at the point of growing up spiritually. None of us expect to find answers, really. We are here to learn. Our restless questions lead us on to our own glimpses of the truth, which is more than many-faceted; it is infinitely varied without ceasing to be one. And we seem to know that keeping each other's company is the way to do this. Each of us is grinding a lens of pure quality, and I have no doubt—none whatsoever—that we will succeed.

Letting Go

You've probably heard this one before, but please try to laugh anyway:

> *A man falls from a cliff and just manages to catch hold of a thin root growing out of the rocks. He is hanging, dangling above certain death, and although he is not religious, he calls out to the heavens, "Help! Is there anybody up there?" A voice responds: "Yes my son, I hear you. Let go of the branch and I will catch you." The man thinks for a minute, looks down at the rocks below and then shouts, "Is there anybody else up there?"*

    I think we laugh, as always, because we can identify with the central character. It may even be that we also feel that life is a slender root on which we are hanging for as long as our grip will endure, and we sometimes want to call out with the same question. As somebody remarked about being condemned to hang, there's nothing better to concentrate the mind. But the answer is confusing, terrifying. Let go? Not on your life, mate. My mama didn't raise no fool. If I let go of this branch, I'll fall. I learned that when I was learning to walk—one hand on the coffee table and two feet on the ground. It's been a basic law of nature since Newton's head had a conjunction with the apple. Letting go is curtains.
    And yet, life as we have always lived it is one long series of letting go of things. Maybe we had what is now known as a "Linus blanket," a scrap of cloth that we refused to let go of in infancy. My sister had one. She held on to it like a lifeline, which perhaps it was. I can remember the ruses and plots my parents conceived in order to get her to let it go, if only to wash it. They would try distractions, counter-offers, even threats. Mostly they just ripped it from her fingers and stopped their

ears while she screamed. She managed to hold onto the thing until just before she started school. One day she just dropped it. I saw it lying in the hall. It was just a dirty square of pink blanket, but it had been almost an appendage of my sister's for as long as I'd known her. I showed to my mother and she got rid of it in some mysterious adult fashion. My sister never looked back.

At a certain point you let go of school friends. You're not always aware you're doing it; it's just that some other people enter your life and you go with them. The transition seems smooth in retrospect, but if you'd been faced with the knowledge that you'd have to let them go at the time you would have complained like my sister about her security blanket. One day you leave your childhood home and go to live somewhere else. And one day you leave your family and start one of your own. Each step involved letting go, though it may not have seemed so at the time. Letting go is something we all do.

In my work I've met a lot of people who had to go through an experience of letting go that wasn't so easy, people who have lost partners to divorce or death, people who have been made "redundant," that awful British euphemism for being laid off. A few times I've sat with people who were terminally ill, who were faced with the prospect of the big letting go—letting go of life itself. At those moments something extra enters the mix that you might not expect. People often want to know if it's all right to die. You spend your life looking after yourself, trying to maintain health, and then something finally happens you can't control. It's not so much that you fear death—although, really, who doesn't? It's about giving yourself permission to uncurl your fingers from that slender root on the cliff, to accept the inevitable. And much of what people like me do at hospital bedsides is just that—helping the person let go.

From the earliest moments of our lives, we learn to hang on. The mobile dangling over the cot begs to be handled. We send out one of our clumsy little hands on a sortie, get it all wrong, and cry. When we manage to get hold of something, we don't want to let it go unless there is something else even more intriguing to take hold of. And to a real extent, all of life is like that: swinging from vine to vine but always grasping the next object before letting go of the one we're holding.

Meanwhile we hear strange messages from the heroes of consciousness, people like Jesus and Rumi and the Buddha. They are enjoining us to let go of all those lovely things that make life reasonable: wealth, health, reputation, even family. This is hard to hear. A lot of fundamentalist Christians would have us believe that Jesus actually wants us to have all these things: it's okay to be rich, slim, successful, as long as you read the Bible and support the television evangelists. I've known people who say that Jesus even finds them a parking place every time they go shopping. This from the man who said, "Birds of the air have their nests, foxes have their holes, but the Son of Man has nowhere to lay his head." The same guy who refused to speak to his mother when she was complaining about his work.

The Buddha? Give it all up; it's just illusion anyway. Beg for your dinner, wrap yourself in a simple cloth, sleep under trees. Let go of what you so happily call reality in order to find the real. Rumi? Well, he's reported to have said that you can't set foot on the spiritual path until you've been chased out of town as a madman. That's taking "letting go" very seriously indeed. The Sanskrit for it is a little tune that friends of the Indian teacher Meher Baba used to sing: *Jane do, jane do*—let it go, let it go.

Of course, there are times when not letting go is the right thing to do. You can't practise detachment with someone else's life. You can't refuse to send your kids to school or buy them medicines just because you want to transcend your limited ego. You can't let invaders have their way with innocent civilians in the quest for personal detachment. You can't sit by and watch as ruin happens needlessly, whether to the environment, to abused minorities, or to children. Letting go is personal: it has to be about your own life.

Letting go is often seen as cruel or wrong by others with whom you are involved. A marriage ends because one partner wants to change, for example. There is a lot of that going around these days. When I'm called upon to work with people in that situation, there are just a few things I want to know: is the changing person being honest? Are they sure? And have all reasonable avenues been pursued? If they have, if the person has really put all this to the test, then there is nothing to do but bless them. To do otherwise is to conspire in a falsehood.

What about the other partner, one might ask? Is it fair that they should have to let go because of the other's decision? Well? Here's what I have had to conclude: the object of their grasping has already gone, in all but name, anyway. What remains is the task of helping the other to let go in a way that is beneficial and leads on to growth and understanding. There is no other way. This might sound simplistic, but I ask you to think of your own experiences of this situation, and I think you'll agree.

Things change. We might want, because we're just human, after all, to conspire in a fantasy that things will always be the same as they are right now. We all do it. We make little shrines in our homes, fill photograph albums with magic charms that have fixed a moment in vanishing time. I once asked a guy who buys entire lives—all the furniture, books, and mementoes of someone who has died—what happens to all the photographs. He just grunted, "What do you think? We burn them." That might bring you up short next time the snapshots come back from the photo lab. You can't really immortalise someone in celluloid.

But I'm focussing on the bad news here. There is good news, too. To find it, we have to go right back to the joke at the beginning of this chapter, where we left the poor guy hanging off the cliff. There's another story that's eerily similar. This one comes from the Zen tradition:

> *A man has fallen from a cliff and hangs dangling by a root. Below is a drop of hundreds of feet, and certain death. He can only hang on for so long; he must inevitably let go. He looks about and sees a wild strawberry growing from the rocks. He plucks it and eats it and says, "Ahhh, how sweet!"*

It may be difficult to imagine enjoying that strawberry very much, what with all the gravity problems you've got. But the story is used as a metaphor for life as it really is. Whether we want to accept it or not, we are indeed on that cliff face. If we want to engage in fanciful dialogue with the heavens, that is fine. But while we're doing so, we wouldn't want to miss that strawberry, the sweetest one in the world.

The truth is, we don't know what will happen to either chap when they let go of the root. We can speculate, but until we are at the point of letting go ourselves, we cannot know. What we can do is listen to those who practised letting go while they lived, the same ones we talked about earlier, the heroes of consciousness from all traditions who spent their lives on that cliff.

What they all seem to be saying is that the fleeting and insecure nature of life is not tragic but paradoxically wonderful. They don't say that they will catch you when you let go nearly so much as say there is a reality that underlies the hanging, dangling temporary security of our projects, and that that reality can be encountered only by letting go of false hopes. Far from swooping down to remove you from the peril of the slender root, they will dare you with love to go there again and again until you experience the truth. And they will tell you this: you have already let go, whether you know it or not. You did it when you first drew breath, and you will do it with your last. That is what life is all about. That is how you move from the plaintive question, "Is there anybody else up there?" to the simple, fulfilling statement, "Ahh, how sweet!"

So What?

Not long ago I spent a few weeks in the mountains of Spain. I had a long time in which to obey the Spanish proverb about life: *Es bueno no hacer nada y luego descansar.* "It's a good thing to do nothing at all, and then have a rest."

But, of course, I wasn't really doing nothing. I might have been reclining a bit more than usual, but my mind wasn't really having it. Stretched out beside a river is when things you try to outrun by being busy all the time catch up with you. So if I looked at the cool water rushing by, I was nabbed by Heraclites' saying, "You can't put your foot in the same river twice." Meaning: everything changes; nothing is permanent. Under an olive tree, I became aware that Plato's *academe* was actually an olive grove. And so life, the universe, and everything tracked me down, and—surprise, surprise—I philosophised and sermonised. Oh well, as the song says, "You can run, but you can't hide."

One of the things that seemed to be nagging at me was the return of an old problem. I refer to this problem by the code name, *So what?*

So what? is what you say when you want to dismiss a situation as irrelevant or a question as pointless. Teenagers are notoriously adept at employing this tactic when they are debunking adult values. So you worked very hard and got a good grade, or a big car, or a knighthood? *So what?* The beat generation, strangling on an overdose of existentialism, used to say *So what?* about almost everything. This was called nihilism, but for many of us, it was just a way of sounding cool. When you say *So what?* you are fending off meaning, putting yourself out of the reach of issues that clamour in our psyches for attention. It's an updated version of those lines of Ecclesiastes: "Vanity, vanity; all is vanity."

So what? worked its way into my theological thinking during my holiday reflections. I was thinking that from the time you are born, you are faced with unanswerable questions. Why is the sky blue, Daddy? How does eating make you get bigger? Where did my hamster go when it died? And then the sophistication level deepens: How will I know when I'm in love? What happens to me when I die? Is there a God?

And so we respond by making personal formulations of meaning. We develop a theology, or an anti-theology, if you like. "There is no God; that's a myth for savages and little children." Or we buy into one of a number of religious options, from born-again Christianity to Zen Buddhism, and we try to make the stubborn random elements of life fit the pattern. We link this to the big question, the first one that springs to the lips when religion is mentioned: Is death the end? We cannot say that we *know*, only that we believe, or try to believe. And meanwhile, our lives go spinning along, hurtling us toward the mystery of personal extinction. Whether we are a Zoroastrian or a druid, a cynical atheist or a dervish dancer, we die.

There are those who say that it doesn't much matter if what you believe is true or not, as long as it gives you comfort. As in the hollow pronouncement of the genius Karl Marx, it is only an opiate, like booze, fanaticism, and the craving for fame and glory. As far as this metaphor goes, it's perfectly true. That is, belief itself doesn't change anything. So if belief is only as far as religion takes us, it deserves the reply: *So what?* You live, you believe something or nothing, and then you die.

Sometimes people are lucky enough to experience—as opposed merely to believe—that there is something beyond and within all this that gives it purpose and meaning. This is known as a mystical experience, and it's more common than you might think. It is often called transcendent, and it gives rise to a different kind of belief. People can have this with a near-death experience on an operating table, during a walk in the mountains, or on first glimpse of a beloved child. I would be surprised to hear that there is anyone who has never had something comparable. If it were not so, I suspect you wouldn't be reading this page.

This kind of experience is timeless and very real while it happens, but then it fades and may become a memory, like all the others we store away. There is one important difference, though. This memory of a transcendent reality is likely to emerge whenever the question of death is present. It has no tenets; that is, it doesn't necessarily translate into theology. It doesn't have logical sequences or rules It is simply a kind of balancing experience to the one we usually inhabit. I was lucky enough to have had one such experience as a young man. I won't give you the details now. In the first place, it was very personal, and in the second, you can probably fill in the gaps from your own experience. In my case, it came after a long and intense period of searching and a great deal of reading, as well as the ingestion of mind-altering substances and several trips to India. When it came, it quite literally knocked me to the floor. This was on a serene Tuesday morning in India when I had ingested nothing more potent than a hard-boiled egg and a cup of tea.

As I recovered from the intensity of the experience—if you have had something similar, you will know that there is no other way to describe it than by saying "recovered"—I had a single idea. I thought, "Art, send yourself a telegram (nowadays, I suppose, an email) into the future. Tell yourself what has happened and remind yourself that when the doubts start to gather again, when the inevitable flattening of mere life gets to you, that there was at least one moment in which you knew that everything in the universe was singing the same song and that nothing is ever lost."

And so I did. And after that, the search was in some respects over. But in case you're wondering—and it would be very kind of you if you were—I had not become a God-realised being. I was neither a guru, nor holy, nor even less restless. I had no fewer problems, no less anxiety, no fewer unhealthy appetites, no less of a need to get on with the rest of my life. What had changed was that I stopped devouring Herman Hesse and D. T. Suzuki and Alan Watts, stopped buying paperback books that told me how to practise karmic regression in my own living room, stopped putting the same emphasis on astrology, numerology, and the *I Ching*. It seemed to me that I had realised that, in terms of the big question of life and death, I was secure. I felt that I could say that I knew that God, or the Ultimate Reality—call it what you will—did exist. That in the final analysis, everything is all right.

End of story, right? Wrong.

That's what was bugging me on my vacation in Spain. It comes down once again to that old question about the value of belief. I have *believed* since that day in India, and even when things have been bad since then, that belief has persisted. It's probably why I had the nerve to try to practise the impossible job of ministry; it's a part of who I am. But sitting by that river in the Sierra Nevada, the question came up again: *So what?*

So what? in this case meant something like this: I have a belief that might well sustain me in times of trouble. I fear death, like everyone, but then again I fear jumping into cold water, too. I don't concern myself with life after death, because I believe that life and death are the same thing, that nothing is ever born and that nothing ever dies. Don't ask, please; I couldn't explain that if I tried. So what's missing? What is there *beyond belief* that needs exploration?

The mystics and sages of all cultures—read them for yourselves—seem to have something in common. Many of them speak of a kind of restlessness that takes them over once they have had an encounter with a transcendent reality. This is where the metaphorical sheep are separated from the goats. Unlike those who are content to wait out life, knowing that it has, in one sense, at least, a happy ending, the great ones begin the search in earnest.

The examples are too numerous to mention, but taking one each from the Christian and the Islamic mystical traditions, we can see this clearly in the lives and work of Saint Teresa of Avila and J'allahudin Rumi, the founder of what we now know as Sufism. Though they came from very different traditions, they were roughly contemporaries.

Both expressed their inner experiences in metaphor, as an "interior castle" and as a "tavern." Both told of a kind of romance that existed between God and themselves personally. Teresa once spoke to her inner vision of Jesus and complained of the rigours that her longing for union had put her through. The figure of Jesus answered, "I treat all my friends this way." To this, Teresa replied, "No wonder you have so few."

Rumi spoke of the intense longing for what he called the "tavern keeper." This was the personified One of whom we are all part, and to whom we return through a long, divine "romance." The metaphor of the tavern and of the drinking of wine—forbidden by Islamic Sharia law—expressed the strong feeling of longing for contact with the divine. In both cases, the path to union took off where the simplicity of belief ended.

I think that is why I was giving myself such a hard time by the river in the last couple of weeks. Something about my belief had begun to bother me. It had begun to seem that my religious conviction was a little smug; that it could be accused of accommodating a personal copout. It might be that some form of that same restlessness was beginning to affect me. I thought that it's not enough simply to believe; you have to want to experience, to *become*.

I said to myself, "Okay, you have religious beliefs. You're not worried about the ultimate shape of things and what happens after death. But how is that belief affecting your life? Where does it become ethics and morality? What does it mean about how you must live in relation to others? What's the point of belief if it doesn't translate into a new way of being?" In other words, *So what?*

It began to occur to me that what lies beyond belief is *action*. I don't mean merely studying theology (which I have done) or even necessarily doing projects for the benefit of humanity (which I also have tried). I mean something more like trying to make sense of my life in terms of what I purport to know. To realise, in the sense of *to make real*. And it seemed to me that my insights had been only partial, that I had taken the awareness of the final *all-rightness* of the universe as an invitation to just hang around. It was little more than a kind of cosmic insurance policy.

Those whose awareness goes beyond mere belief can't just sit still with it. As Teresa and Rumi would have us know, it's a bit like being in love: something is implied; something must be done. Something about the truth demands its expression. I believe that is why we have it. If the universe is alive, conscious, and made of love, then that reality demands to be lived, not just recorded And it seems to me that in time it will find its way from cold storage in the mind into the active work of the heart, changing from a private treasure into a public asset.

What that means in terms of day-to-day living is still unclear. In the case of spiritual heroes like the Rabbi Jesus, it meant becoming the first citizen of a different kind of world. In the cases of countless sages, it meant leading a life solely by the dictates of the awakened heart. But for ordinary folks like you and me, it will probably take somewhat humbler forms. I know now that there is something I ought to do about it, and if I discover what that is, I'll let you know.

If There Was a God...

Here's something you might not know. What do you think was the happiest day of the year for a transvestite in New York City back in the sixties? Yes, that's right. It was Halloween, because that was the only day of the year when they could cross-dress in safety from prosecution. They could exchange their saddle oxfords for stiletto heels and their ties for tiaras, and no one could stop them. It must have been a relief.

I'm no transvestite, but I think I can understand how they felt. It must have been as though there were this one magical time when the rules seemed suspended and something frustrated in them was permitted to manifest. One season of the year is like that for me. At Christmastime, the hard boundaries of belief are suspended. It's a time for talking animals and flying reindeer, for elves and angels, and for a friendly fat man to squeeze down chimneys. It's also the time when a miraculous birth, heralded by a star, took place in a stable.

It's not so much that we believe any of those things. It's that we can feel a certain fondness for the unbelievable. If we can get in touch with the child that still lives in some dark corner of ourselves, swaddled in cherished myths, we can take a real holiday from the rough slog of remaining serious and grown-up all the time. You don't have to be a closet Christian to experience this. You can be Jewish, Muslim, Hindu, or nothing at all and still feel a shift in attitude, if you will. All you need is a dose of childlike wonder to suspend your attitudes for a while.

The attitudes we have to shift are hard ones. They have been formed over many years by enduring mere reality. They are so close to who we have become that we may not even be able to see them any more. They protect us from gullibility and therefore vulnerability. But they also imprison us in their self-limiting loops of logic and control. And I believe that they blinker our eyes from what any child will tell you is a landscape strewn with miracles.

The hardest of these attitudes is something we all have in good measure: to one extent or another, we are all sometimes atheists. An atheist, unlike a good old agnostic, is not unsure about the existence of God. An atheist may be unsure about many things, but on that score, they are firm: there is no God. Nobody is immune from this hard little idea that creeps into our minds, probably not even the pope. What is wonderful about it is that we are willing to be unsure about all sorts of things: astrology, life on other planets, even ghosts; but about God, we are sure. Sure, that is, until some event sends us into casualty at three in the morning or we find a lump where there should be no lump. As someone said, there are no atheists in foxholes. There are times when a prayer wells up inside us without volition and we are willing to put aside unbelief.

But I have come to think that we should have other holidays from our unbelief, not just those awful ones that try our spirits. Just as every New York drag queen needs Halloween, every atheist among us needs Christmas. So next time it rolls around I invite you to spend a few minutes away from your theories and hard-won scepticism. I invite you to imagine what it would be like to have a naïve faith in God. I know it seems silly, even useless. But, if you'll come with me on this little exercise, I'll give you a magic charm to protect you from gullibility. It's one small word, but it opens up a universe of possibility. After this chapter you can fold it up and put it back where you always keep it—in the crowded collection of words in your head. The word is "if."

If there was[5] a God, he wouldn't look like the old guy on the roof of the Sistine Chapel. Unless, of course, you are a white-bearded old man yourself. Because if there was a God, he would look a lot like you. That's because he wouldn't be found in the sky, riding in on clouds of glory, but inside your deepest self. The deepest self wouldn't be the familiar, shop-worn personality we present to the world, but a self that

---

5. I know: "were" is correct, but "was" is what we all say, isn't it?

is in all things. This self would be who we truly are, even though we're not aware of it. This self would mostly be hidden from our minds because they are always busy just being what we seem to be.

Sometimes, while watching a sunset or catching a glimpse of a newborn baby, the self would leak through the screen for an instant. Just a flash, but one that would have a lot to tell us before we shut the curtains again. The self wouldn't have any great words to say, because the self would appear inside our little selves. It might leave behind that feeling that we call awe, or an intuition of great love and peace. It wouldn't matter that this is what people call mystical experience, because those are just words. It would be a feeling of something very familiar, even though foreign to our usual way of looking at things. If there was a God, this is the way he would appear.

If there was a God, she wouldn't have any rules. There wouldn't be any things you had to do that ran contrary to your nature. She wouldn't be impressed if you spent hours on your knees, took vows of chastity, or wore a hair shirt. She wouldn't be in the business of passing out gold stars for attendance at church, either. In fact, she may be less likely to appear in a church at all if you were trying to force yourself into an attitude of piety. She would seem very capricious, even fickle, because when you acted with stubborn compliance to rules handed down by people whose desire was to cage her inside their doctrine, you would be missing the point.

On questions of morality, God would be difficult to pin down. What seemed like a good thing to do in one situation wouldn't work in another. That's because she would really have only one principle: what makes you sense her presence is what we call "good" and that which estranges her is what we call "evil." If you set out to impress her by helping the poor, giving money as a kind of bribe for her favours, she wouldn't send down a lightning bolt; she'd probably just yawn. If, on the other hand, you felt a spontaneous concern for someone other than yourself, and without thinking made a gesture of generosity or support, she'd stir in your heart for an instant, and the self that you really are would show itself a tiny bit.

If there was a God, he wouldn't pay much attention to routine prayers and even less to rituals. He would snore through organ music, unless the soul was touched by it, and he'd say, "No, thanks" to blessed bread and wine, unless the act became an occasion of spontaneous worship. He'd be more likely to pay attention to what you did when you gave up your seat on the bus to somebody that needed it than how many metres of carpet your knees had touched in cathedrals. He would be maddeningly hard to contact from the phone box of your daily prayers, but then show up unexpectedly in the strangest places, like the pub. If there was a God, he would say that he was only contactable when you were out. Where the false self holds sway, God is a truant. All the prayer in the world, all the flattering words and pious assertions wouldn't break through the busy signal on the other end of the line.

If there was a God, she would be most visible in the presence of love. That's because love is the sticking plaster the holds the universe together. Love is the gravity that holds the constellations in their patterns, the force that makes creatures want to mate, the basic stuff of all human happiness. God wouldn't be interested in fear, which is love's opposite, so all that careful flattery meant to prevent disease and earthquakes would turn her off. She might have been tolerant of our ancestors bowing down in front of graven images, but by now she'd expect us to know a bit more. That would be because there have been so many among us from all parts of the world who got to know her well, and they have filled books with their experiences. All these people said the same thing: "God is love." And, inversely, love is God, and where it appears, she does.

If there was a God, he wouldn't place much emphasis on death. He would understand how we cling to the apparent safety of the tissues and fluids that make up our bodies. Knowing that we cannot know that we are more than flesh, he would often make an entrance at deathbed scenes, when our hopes of keeping the old pump running have just about disappeared. He would give us clues, even though we ignore them. He would give us plenty of evidence that once we lay in a water-filled sac and grew ourselves bodies in order to experience the physical world. He would give us recurrent signs that the body contains who we really are for a time, but in order to recall our origins, the body becomes once again mere stuff.

He would send us little messages all the time, despite our failing eyesight and loosening teeth. He would be very close in times of suffering, because that is the nearest place in the inner orbit to seeing him. He would be patient with our bargaining and evasive behaviour, smile lovingly as we set about to engineer longer terms in the body through science, but, also lovingly, he would also make sure that we didn't miss out on our opportunities—any opportunities—to make his acquaintance. He would know that the suffering of others often made us more superstitious than compassionate, but he would be there near those whose spontaneous caring brought them to the bedsides of the afflicted. That's because when love wins over fear, he would be around.

If there was a God, she would have a sense of humour. In fact, when the pure absurdity of things bubbled over into that mysterious act of laughter, she would be as near as our own breath. The seeing of the cosmic joke that underlies the melodrama of our stories would be holy—whole making. She would know that when we laugh—really laugh, not just snigger or sneer—we come to know her in her role as playmate and friend. Solemn worship would be less attractive than fun, where she could be glimpsed as a social companion rather than remote danger. That is why she would so often be found in the company of children.

If there was a God, she would make sure that whatever happened had a purpose. Not a selfish motive of domination and control, as so many of our ancestors thought, projecting their own base natures skyward. Not a hard law of retribution or machine-like operation of cause and effect, either. She would set the table with our gifts and opportunities and invite us to the feast. We could eat salad and sprouts and complex carbohydrates with lots of fibre, or we could stuff ourselves on cake, and that would be all right, too. The invitation would be to nourish ourselves, to grow up strong and wise, and in time, a whole lot of time, we would. Craving, avoiding, dieting, and gorging would all convey their meaning. God would be there, because she would always be there, inside, and making sure that, in one way or another, we'd all get what we need.

If there was a God, the time would come when we'd be aware of him pretty much all the time. As we did that we would change, because the lures and necessities of life would become less important. The self inside would occupy more and more of our lives until there wasn't very much left of our little selves. People would notice, and those who had acquired a taste for the invisible would follow us around. If we got really far along this path, somebody might crucify us or build a statue of us or make a new religion. This would be all right as long as people understood what was happening, but in time it would become a silly magic show put on in a lot of presumptuous buildings, everybody would start making exclusive claims on the truth, and God would have to appear somewhere else.

If there was a God, he would know it isn't easy to be spontaneously holy. It isn't easy to love, either—that comes with a lot of practice. He would realise that it all seemed hopeless, even if you believed in it. So he'd tell you to do one thing, something anyone could do. He'd tell you to remember him. Just that. Not love him, because sometimes you can't. Not believe him, because that is next to impossible. Not spend hours tormenting yourself with his absence, because this only drives him further away. Not getting degrees in theology or preaching sermons. No, I think he'd say, "Remember me." And in time, that would be enough.

If there was a God, I might feel I had to write a book about it.

What I Wish
I Had Said to Mary

My stepdaughter Mary was about six years old when she came to me holding a tiny object. She had been playing in the front garden and found what appeared to be a cut gemstone. She opened her fist slowly to reveal it.

"Is it real?" she asked in a quavering voice.

It looked to me like a badly made glass stone from a costume jewellery ring. I held it as solemnly as I could up to the light. I was stalling, because I didn't know how to answer her. If I had said, "No, dear, it's just glass," I would have been telling the truth, something upon which I place a fairly high value. But then that look of childish wonder, poised on the razor's edge between reality and fantasy, would disappear from her face. If I had told her the stone was real, on the other hand, I would have been setting her up for a fall later. That felt too much like betrayal. I couldn't even say I didn't know, because I did.

I don't remember what I said. It was probably one of those trick answers adults use when they are stumped. Something like, "It's very pretty dear. Now go and help Mummy with the flowerbed. There's a good girl."

The other day I realised what I should have said. Too bad we don't get a second chance, and by the time we are wiser the grownup children are making their own mistakes. Because it matters what we say to one another. It matters a lot.

I could have said, "Look, I'll tell you what. Bring me a little box, a matchbox, or something. You can colour it with your crayons and stick little stars on it. Then we'll find some cotton and put the stone carefully inside. Then you take it and hide it somewhere safe, where only you know where it is. Next year at this time, we'll open it, and then you'll know whether it's real or not."

That's what I wish I'd said to Mary. Maybe that's what I would like to say to everybody. When something comes along that might be important, however irrational that might be, don't get carried away, but don't explain it away, either. Put it somewhere safe, until the world has revolved enough times that you may be ready to understand what it is you have found. Then take it out, examine it closely, and reap the benefits of your search.

Remember: the truth doesn't change. You do.

The End

0-595-28395-0